COLLIDING
WITH
THE CALL

WHEN FOLLOWING GOD TAKES
YOU TO THE WILDERNESS

CORELLA ROBERTS

Dedicated to Mom and Dad,
who never once suggested I abandon the call.

CONTENTS

Acknowledgments

I CAN'T POSSIBLY GIVE adequate thanks to all those that have, in one way or another, been influential to this book and my heart carried onto its pages. But here are just a few that must be said.

Troy. You've been by my side through it all. We've wrestled with the call together, struggled to make sense of the journey together, and walked closer to Jesus together. This book wouldn't be here without your sacrifice and support. Thank you, my love.

Mom, you've been a cheerleader, an editor, a sounding board, a marketing strategist, a distribution manager, a prayer warrior, and more. You're simply the best.

Elizabeth Lumkes, fellow writer and dear encourager. How grateful I am for the heart you put into the reading of my early manuscript.

Angela Trusty, thank you for teaching me a new use for semicolons.

Hannah Willis, artist extraordinaire and friend. Thank you for making my imagination take shape.

Kyounga, Ross, and Shane, thanks for your generously donated skill and time.

To all my Alaska and Thailand friends, whether named or not in this book, you are part of the story. You are part of my heart. You are part of God's work in me. I treasure your friendship and the memories we've shared more than you know.

"This is what the Lord has commanded: 'Take an omer of manna and keep it for the generations to come, so they can see the bread I gave you to eat in the wilderness when I brought you out of Egypt.'"

—EXODUS 16:32

Father, this is my omer of manna. May it be to your glory.

Introduction

"GOD, WHAT IS THIS PLACE? I thought you called me here, but now I don't know."

Eleven years ago, I stared out the window of the duplex we rented from our school district in rural Alaska, tears streaming down my cheeks like the never-ending rain that pelted the glass, blurring my view of the pristine lake and mountains beyond; and I wondered how it was possible that God had abandoned me in this place of obedience to Him. If I was following His will for my life, how could I be so miserable? Where was the abundant life? Where was the fruit? Where was Jesus in the storm?

I had answered the call. The call to serve. The call to obey. The call to lay down my life and let God use it for His glory.

> "This is how we know what love is: Jesus Christ
> laid down his life for us. And we ought to lay down
> our lives for our brothers and sisters."
> 1 JOHN 3:16

So, what went wrong? Early on in my life with Christ, I internalized the message that I would only be happy inside of God's will.

1

But I was anything but happy.

This journal entry—one of the few where I let myself be truly transparent—shows a bit of my anguish:

> I'm afraid. Afraid of staying, afraid of quitting, afraid of this time of testing, afraid of failing, afraid of cracking under the pressure, afraid of rebelling, afraid of disappointing everyone, and afraid of my fickle heart, which currently wants a comfortable, familiar life over one full of risks while serving God. Where is my faith? God, help me!

My husband and I slogged through that first teaching assignment filled with shocking disappointment and trauma, and later found restoration and redemption through a fresh start in a new Alaskan village; but still, God needed to show us that we had in no way arrived. All our trying, our doing, our obeying, our serving managed to bring a certain amount of ministry "success"; but it led my heart farther away from the heart of my Father. My Friend.

That step of faith into obedience was so good, a precious gift to my Savior, but also so . . . not what I thought it would be. I found myself standing with the disciples, watching as Jesus' battered, limp body was sealed in a tomb, and with it, all my hopes and dreams for the part I was going to play in His kingdom. It didn't feel like Sunday would ever come, despite His obvious promises.

So, what is a frustrated, bewildered, exhausted disciple to do? Do you throw in the towel that you once so eagerly wrapped about your waist to wipe another's feet? Do you charge ahead, swinging that sickle with greater gusto, determined to find a harvest in a field of stones? Do you cast off the mantle of ministry and return to your weekly position in the third row from the back, slightly to the left of the pulpit, seeking more knowledge, more training, more *something* to make you enough? Or is there another way?

It took a change of continents and a frightening collision with my depravity before I realized I had been scrambling back and forth inside a massive wall. Jesus stood at the only way out, but the key he offered me was frightening. I had built this wall, locking myself away on the inside where I would be sheltered from the pain. The problem was, I was also shunning the joy. If I accepted the key, it meant acknowledging that I was hurt, burnt out, and helpless to restore myself. Only intimacy with the Almighty could bring me back to life again.

My faith journey is not unique. It just might be your story, too. I invite you to walk with me through the desolation of the Alaskan tundra to the stifling heat of a Thai market, finding where God is at work in our hearts along the way. Because in the end, the Author and Perfecter of our faith is more concerned with calling us to Himself than to any place or any ministry or any work for His kingdom.

What is this place? It's both tomb and womb. And it's right where God wants you.

Part 1

THE CALL

"God did not direct His call to Isaiah—Isaiah overheard God saying, ". . . who will go for Us?" The call of God is not just for a select few but for everyone. Whether I hear God's call or not depends on the condition of my ears, and exactly what I hear depends upon my spiritual attitude."

— Oswald Chambers, MY UTMOST
FOR HIS HIGHEST[1]

Open Ears

TROY AND I WALKED HAND in hand out of the lecture hall and toward the underground tunnel that led to the cafeteria. The speaker's challenge still reverberated in my heart.

"What do you think about using teaching as missions after we graduate ... after we get married?" I asked.

He smirked at the playful nudge toward our inevitable engagement and replied, "I don't know. It sounds pretty amazing. I like the idea of teaching in a country that's closed to traditional missionaries."

I nodded. The several short-term mission trips we'd been on had confirmed in both of our hearts a passion to carry the gospel of Christ to unreached parts of the planet. His was an evangelistic bent, mine a compassion bent. But we knew we were compatible. Five years of dating had proven as much.

My imagination raced forward, placing us at an International school in the Middle East, loving families through teaching their children, melding with the local culture to such a degree that we built relationships with the nationals and they asked us about our faith. I could see us raising bilingual children who also exemplified the love of Jesus. It would have its difficulties and dangers, sure, but God would be with us. He promised His presence to those who go for His sake, and that was all I needed to know.

God, if you want to use us in that way, I'm open! I'm ready! I thought. *Just, please don't send me someplace cold, like Russia.*

This wasn't the first time I'd felt drawn toward missions. I distinctly remember listening to a Wycliffe Bible Translators presentation when I was twelve or so. Shocked to learn of the 1.5 billion people who still have no Bible in their own language, I knew then and there that I couldn't ignore the unreached. And I recall at that time telling God that I'd rather be a missionary than a pastor's wife.

Funny how we like to put conditions on our obedience, isn't it? Sometimes God honors those desires; and other times, I'm pretty sure He laughs. Then He sends us someplace cold. Not quite Russia, but close enough. Most likely, what we think we could never stand is exactly what we need. And His love gives us what we need, not what we want. I'm so grateful.

There are as many different interpretations of what it means to be called by God as there are church denominations. For this book, I'll offer mine:

God calls each and every one of His children to partner with Him in bringing His kingdom to earth as it is in heaven. In that broad call are a billion unique calls, suited to every nuance of character and position on this planet. Those billion specific calls are contained within the second greatest commandment—to love your neighbor as yourself.

That, however, isn't the first commandment or our first calling. I believe that before all else, we are called to God's heart of love where we learn how to both love Him and love others. Just as the first and second greatest commandments are inseparable, so loving God and obeying God are wed. This isn't often the emphasis of those persuasive presentations that recruit us toward serving by stirring our compassion, convincing us we're needed, and assuring us of heavenly rewards. Nothing wrong with all of that, but for me at least, I answered the call of the second commandment ahead of the first.

Graciously, God spared no pains in the pursuit of my sincere affections. He kept calling me back to His heart. Kept showing me a more excellent way, this way of love. And part of the journey to His heart was through the path of the wilderness.

Like the Israelites in Egypt, God called me to belong to Him. He opened the way, through the rending of His body, for me to be freed from my bondage to sin. And He promised me a land flowing with milk and honey. But you likely know what came between the leaving of Egypt and the entering of the Promised Land—the Wilderness. Is it possible that when God calls us, He calls us to walk through the wilderness, too? Allures us there, even?

"Therefore I am now going to allure her;
I will lead her into the wilderness
and speak tenderly to her.
There I will give her back her vineyards,

and will make the Valley of Achor a door of hope.
There she will respond as in the days of her youth,
as in the day she came up out of Egypt."
HOSEA 2:14-15

Yes, I am Gomer, Hosea's unfaithful wife.[1] Prone to
wander away from the Lord in search of other lovers who
will not satisfy. And in the wilderness, my Husband wins
my heart back again, showing me the door of hope.

It comforts me to know how many others have traversed
their own wilderness, too. Jonah, of course, is a classic example of being frustrated with God. In chapter 4 verse 3,
after Ninevah calls on the Lord in repentance and you'd
think Jonah would be celebrating, we find him in utter despair saying, "Now, Lord, take away my life, for it is better
for me to die than to live."

Jeremiah was known as the weeping prophet. He faced
bitter opposition and questioned why the Lord seemed to
be allowing his prophecies to remain unfulfilled. "They
keep saying to me, 'Where is the word of the Lord? Let it
now be fulfilled!' I have not run away from being your
shepherd; you know I have not desired the day of despair.
What passes my lips is open before you. Do not be a terror
to me; you are my refuge in the day of disaster," he cries
out in Jeremiah 17:15-17.

Another well-known example of one who struggled
through a literal and spiritual wilderness is David. None
captures his pain better than Psalm 13:1-2: "How long,

Lord? Will you forget me forever? How long will you hide your face from me? How long must I wrestle with my thoughts and day after day have sorrow in my heart? How long will my enemy triumph over me?"

But there are also some admirable people in more recent history that have confessed to periods of struggle and doubt. Adoniram Judson, pioneer missionary to Burma, faced an incredible amount of difficulty. At one point, after he had been imprisoned and tortured for seventeen months, his wife suddenly died, followed six months later by his infant daughter. "He had a grave dug beside his hut and sat beside it contemplating the stages of the body's dissolution. He retreated for forty days alone into the tiger-infested jungle and wrote in one letter that he felt utter spiritual desolation. 'God is to me the Great Unknown. I believe in him, but I find him not.'"[2]

Charles Spurgeon, known as the "Prince of Preachers" for his wide influence, admitted to doubt and depression. "The pain, the politics, the opposition, and the overwork (as well as bereavements, like that of his young grandson) all affected him deeply, if in waves... [He] once said, 'I could say with Job, "My soul chooseth strangling rather than life" [Job 7:15]. I could readily enough have laid violent hands upon myself, to escape from my misery of spirit.'"[3]

Even Grammy award-winning singer, Mandisa, faced a wilderness of sorrow after a dear friend lost the fight against cancer. "It really sent me into the deepest pit of despair that I have ever been in in my life. I was questioning everything about the goodness of God and why He allows things like this to happen,"[4] Mandisa confessed.

Isn't that just what the wilderness does? It forces us to face the hard questions. It exposes idols and false beliefs. And it can, if we don't pack up and return to Egypt, be the place where God reveals Himself in ways we never dreamed possible. Following Jesus is not easy. He never promised it would be. Yet we still conjure these hopes and dreams and expectations of what serving Him should look like. We make the call adventurous, heroic even. We forget that it's nothing more, nothing less, than a call to Love.

Ears open, eyes squeezed tight, I took a leap of faith and answered the call.

Reflection Questions

What do you think about Oswald Chambers' quote, *"The call of God is not just for a select few but for everyone. Whether I hear God's call or not depends on the condition of my ears, and exactly what I hear depends upon my spiritual attitude."*?

Do you agree with my description of God's call? How do you define the call of God?

Do you believe God's call often includes a time of refining in the wilderness?

Who Holds Tomorrow?

THIS "YES" TO SERVING OVERSEAS wasn't proving as easy to come by as we'd thought. Missions agencies wouldn't take us with our college debt, and international schools wanted at least two years of teaching experience. I wasn't discouraged so much as I was frightened. I didn't want to lose the passion to follow God's calling on our lives, and if we didn't head toward missions right out of college, would we get too comfortable? Would we decide to start a family and lose our nerve to move some place challenging? Sitting around doing a normal teaching job didn't sound at all adventurous, or nearly as God-honoring, as teaching in a foreign country where most of the population had no clue who Jesus really was.

Then one day, as I was waiting in line for another fine college-cafeteria dinner, a short man at a table in the hallway waved a flier at me. "Hi!" he called. "Would you like to learn about missions in Alaska? The bush villages really need people to tell them about Jesus. Are you a teacher or a nurse?"

Alaska certainly didn't appeal to me. It was cold, like Russia, but worse because it was still America. However, nothing else was panning out, so it couldn't hurt to find out a bit more.

Martin introduced himself and told me about the work his organization was doing in the far North. It was a hard place to live, what with the long, dark winters, the isolation of the fly-in-only villages, and the prevalence of substance abuse; but there were whole pockets of people there that had nobody to show them Jesus' love. Traditional missionaries couldn't just land in a village of 50 people and ask for a place to stay—they'd be shoved right back on the airplane—but teachers and health aides were needed and welcome. No experience necessary.

I thanked him, took the flier, and meandered thoughtfully to the back of the dinner line. By the time I found Troy in the cafeteria he'd nearly finished his meal. I handed him the flier.

"Alaska? I'm surprised you'd even consider it." Oh, he knew me so well.

I shrugged. "It seems like it would actually fit. I guess we could at least pray about it. Maybe send that guy, Martin, an email with our questions."

So, we did. And the more we found out, the more we realized that this opportunity was tailor-made for our situation. The schools there were considered low-income, and as paid public-school teachers, we could apply for the government's loan forgiveness program. Finances would be a non-issue; and that was an amazing answer to prayer, considering the tens of thousands of dollars of college debt that we had between the two of us.

It also satisfied Troy's heart to share Christ with those who had little to no opportunity to hear the gospel, and my desire to love on underprivileged kids. Sure, they might speak English, but many of them lived in physical, emotional, and spiritual poverty. Our hearts were stirred, and we agreed to take a trip up there after our wedding in the summer in order to see firsthand if this was God's path for us.

How many times have I labored over how to determine what God is calling me to do? At least as many times as I've faced a change of direction. I always want God to make it obvious. I want blazing neon signs pointing the way and giant roadblocks in the wrong direction. I want open doors, and just one more confirmation, please. Or a speaking, burning bush. I'd settle for that.

So, when I look back on this introduction to Alaska, I'm shocked to see just how clear it really was. Aside from staying in Minnesota, it really was the only option.

The smart people out there who write about determining God's leading in your life (I may or may not have read the same blog on this topic repeatedly over the years), say that there's a sort of predictable formula to determining your calling. Yes, God's direct leading weighs in; but so do a lot of other factors, including your desires, your unique giftings and experiences, and the obvious opportunity.

When I think about Moses and that burning bush, I tend to think that God stopped him in his tracks and completely diverted his life course. But if I search deeper into his life story, I see that the desire to free his people was already there, hotly manifested when he killed the Egyptian slave-

17

driver in defense of an Israelite. And I see that he was raised in Pharaoh's palace and would have been fluent in the language and culture of Egyptian royalty. God's directive plus Moses' desire and experience equaled his calling, difficult though it was.

There is a definite word of caution that needs to be mentioned here, though. Just because the desire is there, it doesn't mean it's a God-given desire; and just because the desire isn't there, it doesn't mean you're not supposed to obey. Our hearts can deceive us, but I want to remind you of this: If you regularly submit your heart to Jesus as Lord and ask Him to give you His desires, I truly believe He will.

I remember sitting across from a friend once, who was struggling with wondering if she was doing what God wanted her to do. I had one of those moments where I surprised myself with what I spoke to her and solidified a truth in my own heart. I said, "You're asking God to lead you. It's not like you're rebelling or trying to ignore Him. I really think He's powerful enough to direct your steps taken in faith."

But do I really live into those words? That grip on God's sovereignty and His good intentions toward us is firm when all is well. When life smells like roses and the path is sunlit, our faith holds on. But our fingers get slippery with the sweat of confusion and emotion when life's not so pretty and pleasant. We wonder if we made the right choice, answered the right call, obeyed the right voice. And we gather all our disappointment back up into our own hands, often blaming ourselves; and in our more raw moments, blaming God.

Deep down, I think most of us are afraid we'll mess it all up somehow. I know I was. I used to be so worried about getting it right with God. I probably still am more than I know. I don't want to say God told me to do something if I might be wrong. In the end, though, the root of that fear is self-serving. I don't want to look foolish for doing something that fails or doesn't appear to be blessed by God. I wish it was a holy fear of the Lord that guarded my lips from false claims of God's direction, but most of the time it's more of a fear of man.

If I'm so concerned about my own decisions, then I'm left with the reality that I don't fully trust God's power. I end up asking: What happens if I step forward in faith and fall on my face? Can God pick me back up? Can He even turn my failure into something good for His name's sake?

19

Have you ever felt lost in waiting for God to make His path clear for you?

What factors do you believe should weigh in when you're determining God's call on your life?

Do you agree with this thought: *"You're asking God to lead you. It's not like you're rebelling or trying to ignore Him. I really think He's powerful enough to direct your steps taken in faith."*?

Fish Wheel

THE COPPER RIVER CHURNED BEFORE us, her frigid waters gray with glacial silt, while mountains scraped the background of the sky, their forever-frozen peaks disappearing into the clouds. Time worn pebbles clattered down the path to the riverbank as my feet found their way toward the water's edge, following Troy and the kind man who had shown us his state over the past five days. Spruce trees lent their offering of pine fragrance to mask the odor of fish coming from the blood-stained table nearby.

A contraption made of wood and wire stood in the whirling water, bobbing only slightly against its tether until our friend released it. Then it began to spin, stirred to motion by the river's swift current, baskets dipping in and out of the water, going around and around in search of the oblivious fish that would swim into its trap.

Salmon. Synonymous with gold in the far north. These fish are the primary source of income for dozens of coastal communities and the primary source of protein for dozens more inland communities as they swim upriver to spawn every year. As we stared at the fish wheel, spatters of river sprinkling our shoes, Phil explained its significance. It was community property, lending itself to whoever had the time to check it periodically and harvest the salmon from where they slid into the holding tanks. It couldn't legally be used for profit, only for supplying food for families. Subsistence living. The Alaskan way.

We had learned quite a lot about the Alaskan way on this vision trip. We had flown over turquoise lakes in mountain valleys untouched by human hands, walked Bristol Bay's mucky beach lined with fishing boats, and waited out the fog for the chance to fly north. During this waiting period, our gracious hosts let us stay in their home more days than expected, fed us more meals than expected, and flew us to our next destination later than expected. This was part of the Alaskan way.

When we flew away from the bay and over the tundra in the four-seater airplane, Troy was offered the controls as he sat in the co-pilot's chair. *Oh, dear God, I might be coming to see you soon!* I checked that my seatbelt was secure. But it turned out that our pilot was a good teacher and my husband an apt pupil. I mean, of course. How could I doubt him? Except that we were hundreds of feet in the air, hundreds of miles away from any human on land, hurtling through the sky surrounded by only some thin metal with wings. The miracle of flight is never lost on me, but especially not in this moment. Yet this, too, this come alongside and learn from me attitude, was part of the Alaskan way.

We spent one night in the second village, feeling much more at home in the trees than on the ocean, and we stayed up late into the night talking and laughing with the missionary family that let us stay in their "newlywed suite," a sort of lean-to addition that we couldn't quite stand up in.

22

Another missionary, a single pastor from up the river, stopped in. They fed him, too. We feasted on moose something-or-other, served with the story of the hunt. Oh, this Alaskan way, it was so not me, and yet it resonated with something deep within me. That God-given desire for community, flexibility, working with your hands and feeding your family what the land provides.

There was another side to the Alaskan way that we had yet to see, but of the parts revealed on this trip, we wanted in. We wanted it to become our way, too.

Phil restrained the fish wheel again before it brought in any salmon he would have to throw back, and we walked the forested trail back to the truck. This was the end of our vision trip. The next stop was the airport, and I still had one question I just had to ask.

"So, do you think we have what it takes to teach out here?"

Phil looked at me, nodding in his gentle way of understanding. "I saw you stepping in to help with the cooking and the dishes and the kids. So yeah, I think if you have that servant heart, then you have what it takes."

Seriously? Don't we need some rugged Bear Grylls type ingenuity to survive bush living? Don't we need Joanna Gaines like prowess in the kitchen to turn mundane shelf-staples into nutritious meals? Don't we need a pilot's license or training in small engine repair or at least a hunter's safety certification?

Those things might be helpful, but in all his years of leading our mission organization, Phil recognized the defining characteristic of an Alaskan missionary as simply a servant's heart.

The apostle Paul challenges us to servanthood in this way: "Beloved ones, God has called us to live a life of freedom in the Holy Spirit. But don't view this wonderful freedom as an opportunity to set up a base of operations in the natural realm. Freedom means that we become so completely free of self-indulgence that we become servants of one another, expressing love in all we do." (Galatians 5:13 TPT[1])

I love that. And I need that. When I am free from feeling the need to set myself up to succeed in the natural realm, then I am free to serve in love through the Spirit. In any given situation, I could look around and see a thousand things I could improve at in order to be better prepared to serve. But if it's done in order to build a castle for myself, it comes to nothing more than self-indulgence and self-protection.

I must admit that I am the queen of building castles. God has given me the mind of a learner, or maybe just a parrot; so if I want to succeed at something, I study how it is done well, and I learn to fit that mold. Usually, I'm pretty good at it. I've shielded myself from a lot of failure and rejection this way.

I wonder if you've done that, too? I imagine we all have to some degree, at one time or another. Any successful student knows that all you have to do is figure out what each teacher likes and produce something according to their specifications in order to secure a good grade. Even young children know how to work the parental system. One parent will probably give them that ice cream if they keep begging, but the other one despises begging and will shut down any chance for ice cream for days if they ask a second time. You'd better believe that any five-year-old knows which parent to ask that third or fourth time, and which one not to ask repeatedly. We fit the mold. We build castles. We get the ice cream.

But God offers a different way through freedom in the Spirit. His freedom is bathed in love. And love never fails. His way, more than the Alaskan way, is the only sure path of success.

You could build a super sturdy, perfectly designed fish wheel, and set it in the middle of a river filled with salmon; but if it's not untied to be moved by the current, it will succeed in catching nothing. The love of God, alive in our hearts through the Holy Spirit, is the motivating current that enables us to serve. And in Him we are free. We are untethered. We are able to serve in love.

As we flew out of Alaska, watching her mountains, her glaciers, her coastline and her ways disappear from view, I knew we would be back. And I prayed that the ways of a servant, driven by love, would become my ways, too.

The answer to that prayer would come in wildly unexpected ways.

Reflection Questions

What "ways" or culture have you tried to adapt yourself to?

Do you recognize any castles you've built in the name of preparedness that are really a feeble attempt to protect yourself?

What ways do you see God developing servant-hearted love within you?

Extravagant

I RAISED MY HAND, OFFERING to share first. The other trainees sat back, happy to let someone else break the ice. I looked at the text on my screen, feeling confident that I had captured the essence of a good newsletter through telling a story. Obviously, I love writing. And I love dreaming. This was a fun assignment for me.

I stood and read a moving tale about two children that came seeking refuge at our house one night when their parents were drinking and fighting. I told of us welcoming them, reassuring them, and building a relationship with them that we hoped would one day lead to their acceptance of the gospel. It was a good story, based on the very real statistics of abuse we knew existed in the Alaskan bush. It reflected my heart to be a dynamic force of love in the lives of the kids we would teach. Yet, hidden beneath this fictional narrative lay my desire to worship Jesus big.

The most extravagant gift I could imagine giving to my Lord was a totally surrendered life. At this point, I dreamed that would look like putting up with the cold winters of Alaska, loving hurt children in sacrificial ways, and subjecting ourselves to the nuisance of fundraising, minimal though it was. I would use my teaching as worship.

Whenever we dream, imagining our lives in a grander scale for the Lord's service, our desires get all twisted up

27

with His. God puts a vision in our hearts, but we can't take off the tinted glasses to view it flawlessly. Our broken past, our selfish motives, and the whispers of the world all play into our dreaming. The heart to honor Jesus is there, but our self-importance is almost always inflated in how we envision that playing out.

The gospel of Luke, chapter seven[1] tells us the story of Simon the Pharisee, Jesus his honored guest, and an unnamed, uninvited prostitute. Simon asks Jesus to join him for a dinner banquet. I imagine he thought he was doing a great favor for this upstart teacher from Galilee. I can see Simon commanding his servants to scrub the floors and prepare a lavish feast for Jesus and his disciples. His hospitality would show respect to Jesus, but it would also showcase his own wealth and generosity.

The low table is set, cushions on the floor around it for the guests' comfort, and a special place is reserved for Jesus. Simon's favored friends are invited, too. They will also get to see his open-mindedness in welcoming this teacher, whom the uneducated crowds adored, into his home. These law-abiding friends show up precisely on time.

Jesus, I imagine, is a few minutes late, pausing on his way to heal just one or two more desperate followers.

Simon paces by the door, impatience flushing his cheeks. He does not like to keep his friends waiting. Finally, Jesus comes, laughing at his disciples' antics as they approach the house far too slowly. Simon greets him with a forced smile and immediately shuffles Jesus to a spot

28

EXTRAVAGANT

right next to him at the table. He offers Jesus the privilege
of blessing the bread, and after it is broken, they commence
eating. Platters of roasted fish, bowls of boiled vegetables,
and trays of figs and nuts are passed.

A few polite questions are asked of Jesus. Where would
he travel to next? Did he enjoy the weather this time of
year? Was it true that he had raised a widow's son back to
life? Jesus' answers are a bit vague, leaving their interpre-
tation up to the unsatisfied listener, so conversation
naturally shifts into small groups and the dining area is
filled with pleasant chatter.

Simon has been eager to ask Jesus a question about a
particularly controversial section of the writings of one of
the prophets; and he chews his bread slowly, framing the
question in his mind, when the room abruptly goes silent.

A woman has entered the house. A woman he has
snubbed on the street corners, swinging wide of her winks
and waves. Her dress is cut too low at the top and too high
the bottom, and her hair is uncovered, flowing in dishev-
eled waves over her shoulders.

She hesitates only briefly before picking her way
through the crowded room, her eyes lowered and her jaw
set. Simon is speechless as she approaches him. Her audac-
ity is unheard of. He begins to stand up to rebuke her, to
send her away, back to the streets and the life of sin she
must enjoy; but she skirts around Simon and collapses behind Jesus. Surely this wise teacher, this man people are
calling a prophet, will turn her away.

The woman stares at Jesus' feet, trembling as she clutches an alabaster vial to her overly exposed chest. She dares to glance upward at Jesus' face, and when she meets his gaze, great, silent tears pour from her eyes. She scoots on her knees closer to the Rabbi's feet, sets the jar aside, and tentatively reaches out to cup his dung-smeared, dust-coated foot in her hand. Her tears drip from her nose and chin onto the sole of his foot, leaving muddied paths where they trace his creased skin.

Simon squirms. This unimaginable disgrace is happening right beneath his roof, yet he is helpless to stop it without shaming his guest of honor. This woman, horrid as she is, is serving him; and Jesus must be the one to turn her away. How can he not see that she is a prostitute, defiling him with her touch?

Still weeping, the woman begins to use her hair, her mark of glory, to wipe away her tears and the filth from Jesus' feet. Each time she strokes Jesus' sole with her hair, she plants a tender kiss where there once was grime. Over and over again she weeps, wipes, and worships with a kiss.

The guests are starting to mutter now, and still Jesus has said nothing to end this humiliating display of extravagant servitude. Simon searches the teacher's expression and finds no glimmer of irritation or discomfort. As if sensing his gaze, Jesus looks at Simon.

"I have something to tell you," Jesus says.

Hoping for an explanation of some sort, Simon replies, "Tell me, teacher."

Jesus tells him a story of two men whose debts are for-given—one a small debt, one a great debt. "Now, which of them will love him more?"

Feeling frustrated and embarrassed by the obvious an-swer, Simon replies through gritted teeth, "I suppose the one who had the bigger debt forgiven."

Jesus nods.

At that moment, a loud crack sounds from behind Jesus, and the fragrance of perfume fills the house as the vile is broken open. The prostitute sniffles, her painted eyes a mess of black smeared across her cheeks, and she begins to pour the fragrant oil over Jesus' feet, wiping them once again with her long hair.

Simon stifles a cough at the overpowering scent. To him, it's the stench of sin, this perfume purchased with the money of her shame.

Jesus closes his eyes and breathes deeply.

Without opening his eyes, he speaks again to Simon. "Do you see this woman? I came into your house. You did not give me any water for my feet, but she wet my feet with her tears and wiped them with her hair. You did not give me a kiss, but this woman, from the time I entered, has not stopped kissing my feet. You did not put oil on my head, but she has poured perfume on my feet. Therefore, I tell you, her many sins have been forgiven—as her great love has shown. But whoever has been forgiven little loves lit-tle."

Simon flushes in humiliation.

Jesus turns to the woman still bowing behind him. He places a hand on the side of her head and leans down. "Your sins are forgiven," he says gently to her. "And your faith has saved you. Go in peace."

The former prostitute raises her eyes to Jesus' face, wipes her cheeks, and smiles a hopeful smile. She gathers her skirt and nearly skips out of the house, leaving a fragrant wake of adoration and gratitude.

Simon wishes he could flee out of the house, too. His offering to Jesus had just been demoted to a grain of sand in contrast to this street woman's shoreline of worship.

I always long to see myself in this story as the grateful woman, pouring out everything she had in worship of Jesus, but in reality, I'm much more of a Simon. I offer Jesus something that I think honors him, but secretly it honors me, too. I invite Jesus into my neatly crafted ideas and expect His presence to bless them. I make sure my friends and family can see this beautiful service I am doing for Him.

But it falls short of true worship. Praise that is so other exalting that it is self-abasing is completely out of my usual mode of operation. Perhaps I don't fully understand how much I have been forgiven.

Perhaps I don't really grasp just how worthy Jesus is.

You see, even this unnamed prostitute's extravagant affection, poured out on Jesus, pales in comparison to His perfect beauty and His supreme holiness. The best she could offer was still shackled to her shame and purchased in her sin.

Until Jesus redeemed her worship, it, too, was worthless. But when He spoke life over her sacrifice, over her, he reclaimed it all.

My Savior, this King of Kings and Lord of Lords, the Lamb who was slain, is worthy to receive every bit of praise and honor and glory and wisdom and power and wealth and strength. He is worthy of my best efforts, my bitterest tears, and my most extravagant expression of love. But I must remember—and you, too—*we* must remember, that no act of service and no offering of praise can ever come close to being worthy of our incomparable King.

He alone brings life out of death and beauty out of ashes. He is the extravagant one, not me. Not even a bold prostitute that faced potential rejection and certain humiliation to offer her tears and kisses in sacrificial praise to Jesus. And certainly not an eager elementary teacher, ready to tell the story of a changed Alaska as the result of inviting Jesus into her job there.

Read Luke 7:36-50 three times, each time picturing your-self as a different character: Simon the Pharisee, the prostitute, and Jesus.

What did God reveal to you as you put yourself in the story?

Keep Knocking

STARTING IN JANUARY OF THE year we were hoping to move to Alaska, we started watching the school district webpages for job openings. Finding a small village that had a position for both an elementary teacher and a secondary math teacher might be difficult, but we were hopeful. Based on initial impressions from our vision trip, we were hoping to be more inland than coastal, and given the necessity to be in proximity to other missionaries from our organization, there were only two school districts we were seriously considering.

We emailed each of them a letter of interest, and only one responded. They were confident that they would have positions for us and encouraged us to wait another month until job openings were more certain. While we waited, we learned what we could about the various areas we were interested in, and just for fun, we kept an eye on the openings in the coastal school districts, too.

Teacher contracts were returned, job openings were posted, and there were only two obvious opportunities. Both were coastal, but in different districts. Uncertain which to pursue, we prayed and agreed to go for the one that seemed slightly more intriguing to both of us. Why we thought we preferred that location, I have no clue, but it just appealed to us more. We sent our resumes and waited. And waited. We sent a follow-up email. And waited.

Finally, we determined that the Lord might not be opening that door, so we inquired with the other school district. That was on a Friday. On Monday, they responded, and we set up a telephone interview for Wednesday. By that Friday we were offered the job. One week and done.

We would be two of the four teachers in a K-12 school of about 40 students. Our nearest teammates were a plane ride an hour and a half north of us. The village had one Russian Orthodox church building but no resident priest.

If ever there was an open door, that was it. Just like when God directed us to Alaska rather than the Middle East or Asia, it wasn't the door we thought we wanted open; but it was the only one. He really does make things obvious sometimes.

Troy is known for telling people that if you think God wants you to do something, just start knocking on doors. He's not going to blast your smartphone out of your hand with a door falling from the sky. You have to put it down, get up and take that step to start looking and start knocking. Since the harvest is plentiful but the workers are few, you can be sure that He has some good works prepared for you to do. Just knock.

This is that step into a life of active service for the Lord's kingdom. And it's usually a wobbly step, like a toddler. You've moved from the milk of the gospel into the meat of intentional living for Christ. You might think you're more capable and knowledgeable than you really are, just like that two-year old that says, "I do it myself!" But your Father, just like your earthly dad, celebrates each step taken. And He lets you try, knowing that the lessons you learn through both your successes and your failed attempts contribute to your growth.

Your Heavenly Father can also see who you will become. He knows the end from the beginning. In fact, He's outside of time, so at this very moment in your reality, He is also looking into your eyes, His radiant, redeemed bride, as you enter His joy in heaven. He is both forming you in your mother's womb and dancing with you on the new Earth. To Him, there is no gap between who you are now, in your earthbound, sin-sick body, and who you will be then, in your glorified, shining like the Son resurrected body.

So, we dare not despise these baby steps that get us from *here* to *there*. He is rejoicing over each and every one, even the ones where we trip over the rug, or bang our head on the corner of the table—again. With each step we learn, we grow, and we are that much closer to the full display of His glory.

I believe God made this door into life in Alaska so obviously open for us because He knew the countless times ahead that I would look back and wonder if we made the right choice. It was basically the only choice, so we walked forward in full confidence that God had chosen it for us. That was a confidence I would desperately need to recall in the year ahead.

Reflection Questions

Recall a time you've knocked on a door you thought you wanted God to open only to find it closed. How did you respond?

Recall a time God opened an unexpected door and you walked through it by faith. What was the outcome of that obedience?

Remember not to despise the baby steps that get us from *here* to *there*. Read Zechariah 4:10. What small beginnings is the Lord rejoicing over in you right now?

Part 2

TOUGH OBEDIENCE

I said: "Let me walk in the fields."
He said: "No, walk in the town."
I said: "There are no flowers there."
He said: "No flowers, but a crown."

I said: "But the skies are black;
There is nothing but noise and din."
And He wept as He sent me back –
"There is more," He said; "there is sin."

I said: "But the air is thick,
And fogs are veiling the sun."
He answered: "Yet souls are sick,
And souls in the dark undone!"

I said: "I shall miss the light,
And friends will miss me, they say."
He answered: "Choose tonight
If I am to miss you or they."

COLLIDING WITH THE CALL

I pleaded for time to be given.
He said: "Is it hard to decide?
It will not seem so hard in heaven
To have followed the steps of your Guide."

I cast one look at the fields,
Then set my face to the town;
He said, "My child, do you yield?
Will you leave the flowers for the crown?"

Then into His hand went mine;
And into my heart came He;
And I walk in a light divine,
The path I had feared to see.

— George MacDonald, "OBEDIENCE"[1]

First Landing

EVEN SEATED SHOULDER TO SHOULDER with my husband and two co-workers, conversation was nearly impossible over the drone of the single-propeller airplane, so the four of us spent most of our time peering out the windows, lost in awe.

The Alaska Peninsula sprawled below us. One side flat tundra puddled with amoebic lakes in various hues of brown, red, and green. The other side volcanic mountains, their rocky summits veiled in cloud faces. We watched below for moose, caribou, and bear. When the girls on the opposite side of the plane started gesturing out their window and taking pictures, I tried to peer over their shoulders, but I couldn't get a glimpse of the creature below. Maybe next time.

Finally, the runway came into view. A narrow neck of gravel extended next to the lake, dressed in sleeves of verdant willow bushes. Her rugged crown was the village, made up of no more than 40 wooden houses with one large, gray, tin-roofed building at the center. The school. Soon to become the center of my life, as well.

We bumped our landing into that world on the rough runway, and the four of us—responsible for the education of the entire village—deplaned into a greeting of dogs and smiling Alaskan Natives. Here there was no tarmac beneath our shoes, no advertisement-laden terminal, not even a

41

rough-hewn waiting room. This was the Alaskan wilderness, only faintly scarred by the landing strip.

Fuchsia paint brushes dabbed the only color onto the otherwise green, grey, and blue landscape. Fireweed. So named because this resilient flower blooms best in the soil that has gone through the most assault. Rocky roadsides and burn-scathed hills bear its beauty.

I breathed in the wild, crisp air, savoring its chill on my cheeks.

The two pilots opened the belly hatch and tossed out our luggage along with our wheeled coolers containing the only store-bought fresh food we would have until our next trip "out" two months later. Our Rubbermaid totes of non-perishable food had been shipped from Anchorage and would arrive on the plane sometime in the next week. Hopefully.

The principal introduced us, and a cheerful maintenance man clad in Carhartt's helped us load our lives into the back of the red school pick-up. The canine welcoming committee snarled at each other; and we scuttled into the bed of the truck, beginning our jaunt through the village to the school. We were on the only road in town. Modest single-story houses settled amid the bushes on either side of the road, most of the exteriors made of lumber or plywood, sometimes a mixture of both where an addition had been tacked on. Most homes had an accompanying 4-wheeler, or "Honda," as we would come to call them. Bushes had been hacked away to make space for large satellite dishes, old boats, dog kennels, and piles of firewood.

Suddenly, a boy careened out of a driveway on a bicycle right behind us and pedaled furiously to keep pace. We waved at him and he returned our greeting with a half-smile before disappearing into another driveway. We caught glimpses of a few other children stealing glances at us from their porches, their dark eyes wide with curiosity. I couldn't help but wonder what they thought about this completely new set of teachers. We'd received bits and pieces of information about why all the previous teachers left, but it seemed normal: a new relationship, wanting a change of scenery, deciding not to teach after all. My heart went out to the kids of the village. It's hard to get a solid education and to trust your teachers when none of them stay more than a year or two.

We would be different.

Troy and I envisioned ourselves staying at least five years and really impacting these kids. God had called us to it and opened all the doors. How could it not be amazing? Our hopes were high, and why shouldn't they be? We serve a great God. I knew that much to be true.

The curious thing about hope is that it is literally essential to our survival. I read recently about one teen in northern England who believed so strongly that a simple message of hope could save people on the brink of suicide that she attached uplifting messages to a high bridge that she herself had once thought of jumping from. Some of her encouraging words were: "You are not alone." "Even though things are difficult, your life matters." "You have the power to say, 'This is not how my story will end.'" She offered beautiful threads of hope to those who were hurting. Police say that for six people, that hope was all they needed to step back from the edge and find help.

We love a good story of hope helping someone hold on through a terminal diagnosis, hope reuniting a broken family, hope pushing the juvenile offender to finish college and become a successful business owner, or hope inspiring a rejected coach and his unlikely team to win the State Championship. We love hope's redemptive power. And, of course, it's shown nowhere more clearly than in the face of our resurrected Savior.

Faith, hope, and love will remain, says the apostle Paul. Hope is part of life. A loss of hope is equivalent to death. When hope dies, something always dies with it. To quote a friend of mine, "If you want to know where you are believing a lie, just find the place where hope has died."[1] God brings hope and life. The enemy brings despair and death.

This honeymoon season of obeying the call of God is pregnant with hope. There is something so sweet about embarking on a new adventure with Jesus, hoping that He will do something with your offering of service. This hope sustains you through the difficulties of establishing a new home, a new job, or a new relationship (and quite possibly all of those simultaneously). This hope helps you laugh through cross-cultural blunders or misunderstandings with teammates. This hope fuels your commitment when you're not home when a grandparent passes, a niece is born, or your favorite dog, left to your friend's care, runs away. God sustains us with His hope.

Here's the kicker, though. Diamond-strong hope is formed in the pressure of trials. In Romans 5:3-5, Paul puts it this way, "Not only so, but we also glory in our sufferings, because we know that suffering produces perseverance; perseverance, character; and character, hope. And hope does not put us to shame, because God's love has been poured out into our hearts through the Holy Spirit, who has been given to us."

Glory in our sufferings because it produces the final product of hope? That feels to me like saying, "You wanna be a cowboy? Well, just hold this here rope. See? It's attached to that wild mustang over there. Yup, keep holdin' on. She's gonna drag you through the mud and probably kick you before you finally climb on her back, but once you're up, you'll learn to hang on real tight. Oh sure, you'll get bucked off a time or two, but that'll just toughen you up! Get back on that horse and build your cowboy grit. Once she's tame? Whoo-whee! You will not be disappointed!" I'm sorry, I love horses, but maybe I'll just hire a trainer.

I don't, however, see a substitute for creating strength-filled hope in the Word. Along with Paul's remarkable life of suffering and hope, I see a depressed psalmist cry out repeatedly in Psalm 42 for his soul to stop being so downcast and disturbed and put its hope in God. He tells of lips that will praise in the middle of the suffering and a heart that will hold on to hope in the deep waters.

This is fireweed hope, blooming right in the middle of the scars.

I can be distraught by misplaced hope. I can be disillusioned by deferred hope. But I can never be disappointed by eternity-focused, Spirit-given hope. And, oh, how I hoped my hope was in the right place.

Reflection Questions

When have you come into a situation you knew very little about determined to make a difference? What was the result?

Where has hope died in your life? Ask the Lord to help you identify the lie that is growing there instead.

What scars do you have that have become fertile ground for your strongest hopes?

Love Your Neighbor

OUR TWO-BEDROOM, FURNISHED APARTMENT was just a few steps away from the school and the other teachers' duplex, had a view of the lake and its small beach out the back, and connected to the itinerant counselor's apartment through a shared laundry room. It was quite nice, really, especially by newlywed standards. And it had a real toilet, not a "honey bucket" as we'd heard tell of in teacher housing in the northern-most school districts where permafrost prevented the use of septic systems.

I pulled a framed photo collage out of a tote and frowned. The corner had cracked and separated during shipment. "Troy, do we have any wood glue?"

"I don't think so," he called from the spare bedroom where he was trying to set up our printer.

"I'll check with Stanley."

I stepped into our mud room and knocked on Stanley's door. "Come in!" he hollered. As I opened the door, a haze of smoke and the odor of cooking fish spilled out into the laundry space. Stanley stood at the stove, stirring a curious looking white substance in a pan. He waved me over, dumping the white stuff onto a plate. "Have you ever tried salmon milt?" he asked, offering me a fork.

"Uh, I don't think so. What part of the fish is that?"

"The semen. It's a real delicacy. Try some." He put on his best trust-me-I'm-a-counselor smile.

47

COLLIDING WITH THE CALL

I laughed. "Thanks, but I just wondered if you had any wood glue we could borrow."

He rummaged through a bin by the couch and produced a small bottle. Handing it to me he added, "The girls and Mark are coming over tonight to watch a horror movie— but really it's so bad it's more of a comedy. You guys are welcome to join us."

"I'll talk to Troy. Thanks for the glue." I returned to our apartment, shaking my head at Stanley's quirkiness, yet grateful for his generosity and constantly upbeat demeanor. How he could leave his wife in Montana to fly around between six different villages up here I would never understand, but at least he did it with a smile.

I barely finished gluing the picture frame when I looked out the window to see Christine coming down the boardwalk, her long brown hair blowing across her face in the wind.

"I got all my Disney movies organized and I think I'm only waiting for one more tote with my quilting supplies. My apartment looks pretty good now, but my classroom is still a wreck. How are you doing?" Fresh out of college, Christine was a bundle of enthusiasm, anxiety, and tenderness all mixed together.

"We're still missing three totes, I think, and one of them has our classroom posters. I hope it comes on the plane tomorrow." I had no idea how normal this waiting on the plane would become.

Christine and I chatted for a few minutes, then decided to check in on Jessica. Of the four of us teachers, she had the most experience, but even she hadn't touched thirty yet. She came to Alaska out of the aftermath of Hurricane Katrina and a broken engagement.

Jessica welcomed us in with her gentle, southern drawl; and her yellow lab, Nala, barked nervously before retreating to her kennel. "She's just timid, but she's really sweet once you get to know her," Jessica explained.

Her apartment was immaculate, and the last time I'd poked my head into her classroom, it looked perfect, too. So perfect, in fact, that it made me uneasy.

Along with this core team of teachers, we had an itinerant principal who would visit us for a few days each month and an itinerant Special Education teacher who would also drop in periodically. The rest of the school positions were staffed by locals from the village. Most of them were related to each other, but they had worked at the school for a long time and generally kept family drama away from work. *Generally.* They welcomed us warmly and advised us on some of the sticky situations we would encounter regarding village politics.

There we were, starting a new way of living in a different culture in an isolated bubble. We could close our doors, but we would never be more than a few hundred feet away from one another. We were coworkers, we were neighbors, and we hoped to be friends.

In Leviticus 19:18, God establishes the famous command to love your neighbor as yourself. He reiterates and reestablishes the importance of how we treat our neighbor in numerous ways throughout the Old Testament: don't steal from, don't lie to, don't set traps for your neighbor. Do bless your neighbor with kind words, interest-free borrowing, and the excess produce of your field. (The most repeated rule in this category is to not covet or defile your neighbor's wife. Dare I add that our generation of promiscuous eyes and hearts does just that with an astoundingly flippant indulgence in pornography?)

This command to love your neighbor is again mentioned six times in the gospels and five more times in the epistles. Jesus broadens our definition of a neighbor through his famous parable of the Good Samaritan, demonstrating that neighborly love is not to be reserved for those in close physical proximity, but also lavished on all people in need.

We, however, found ourselves pondering what it truly looked like to love our inescapably close neighbors. Stanley was easy; he felt loved by sharing a meal with him and listening to his wild stories. Christine valued any amount of companionship and time. But Jessica turned out to be a challenge. She didn't really care to eat or visit with us, she occasionally appreciated help in the school but could also be deeply insulted by it, and she definitely didn't want any form of prayer. She called herself an atheist, although she also claimed to hate God for the atrocities she had witnessed. I don't think you can hate someone who doesn't exist, but this was her perceived reality, and no one would convince her otherwise.

As representatives of this God she despised, we soon became targets of her anger, as well. But even in this, Jesus calls us to love: "You have heard that it was said, 'Love your neighbor and hate your enemy.' But I tell you, love your enemies and pray for those who persecute you" (Matt. 5:43-44). My comfortable, American upbringing has shielded me from all but the mildest forms of ridicule. I know nothing of the daily threat many of my brothers and sisters around the world face simply for clinging to the name of Jesus. They're beaten, imprisoned, forced into slave labor and used as sexual objects in order to be shamed. But they still love Jesus, and, by His grace, they love their enemies through prayer.

As difficult as it was, being hated for our faith was a precious glimpse into sharing in the sufferings of Christ and the thousands of martyrs around the world.

I look at where our Western world is headed, and I see a time in the near future where true Christ-followers are not only laughed at for their adherence to the gospel and the truth of the Word, but they are outright hated. How long will it be before holders of a diploma from a Christian university are refused jobs? Before churches are denied the right to rent public facilities or even own property? Before outreach events are forcibly shut down by the authorities and their leaders imprisoned?

Oh, that only happens in countries like China or Pakistan, you might say. America is the land of the free. That couldn't possibly happen here.

But I want to challenge you: What if it does? Will you keep loving your King, even if it feels like all the world will turn against you?

These are the questions we must answer in our hearts now. In the small places of daily ridicule, we are choosing whether or not we will deny our Lord, and whether or not we will take Jesus seriously when he tells us to love our enemies.

That's just awfully hard to do when your enemies don't want your love.

Reflection Questions

What is your heart's response to the reminder of how often the Lord asks us to love our neighbor?

Do you carry any guilt over not loving as well as you think you should? What does God say about those feelings of failure?

Do you hold any pride in how much you've sacrificed to love your neighbor well? What is God saying to you about that?

If you knew you would be rejected for your faith, what would you do? How would you love well?

I Can't Take Your Fish

IN THE WILDERNESS OF ALASKA, everyone learns a bit about living off the land, despite the frequent deliveries of soda and chips. When we weren't creating lessons and trying to figure out the standards-based system we had to teach in, we took the opportunity to get outside and enjoy our stunning surroundings.

The start of the school year marks the beginning of the berry season, and eager children showed us how to crouch in the tundra in search of seedy, dark moss berries and low-bush cranberries. The rare treasure was finding a bush with raspberry-like salmon berries. We preferred to devour our berries fresh and freeze the extras, but the villagers loved to use them in a dish called *akutaq*. Traditionally, *akutaq* was a mix of whale blubber or animal fat and berries. The contemporary version constituted of Crisco, sugar, and berries. It was the sought-after dessert at every potluck.

Our village sat on the edge of a large lake which was drained by a river that fed into the ocean a few miles away. Rugged mountains walled in the lake, changing from green to red to gray with glacial ribbons of white as they ascended; and salmon of all kinds swam up the river to breed in the lake. In other words, it was a fisherman's heaven. Our school janitor offered to take us out in his skiff to the best fishing spots; and although my fishing experience amounted to a few times in a pond and once in the ocean, I knew this wasn't an opportunity to be passed up.

Troy, Christine, and I joined Doug in his small boat, sad that Jessica was too committed to her classroom to step away, and we motored down the river to a rocky beach. Doug patiently taught us how to cast in order to get the flashy lure in front of the aggressive silver salmon, and, before long, we were battling to bring in our first catches. The silvers would jump and splash and put up a fight the whole way to shore. I never did really learn how to fillet a fish, but I'm proud to say that after a couple of weeks I was removing my own hooks and carrying those five to ten-pound fish around by the gills. That was a big accomplishment for a girl who doesn't even like to touch raw meat.

Those memories of fishing on that river are some of the best I have. Out in the boat we often saw fat brown bears and massive bald eagles. We left the cares of school behind and simply enjoyed the beauty and bounty of this incredible piece of the planet. One thing we learned was that our planning and grading could wait, but an invitation to go fishing on a rare sunny day would not.

One day, as we returned to the main beach in front of our apartment with just a couple of fish, another skiff arrived after a day of fishing out in the bay. An old man with a peg-leg hopped out of the boat with a small halibut. He had a sincere grin and said with the faintest lisp, "Well, hey there! Would you teachers like this halibut here?"

Now, I know I'm an anomaly, but I enjoy eating halibut ten times more than salmon, so I sincerely wanted to accept his offer, but how could I? The guy had one leg, for crying out loud. Could I seriously take the only small fish he'd caught after an entire day on the water?

Before Troy could say a word, my pride spoke. "Oh, no thank you. That's really kind, though."

"You sure?" He replied with a bit of a mischievous smile. "These small ones are the best."

I shook my head, thanked him again, and we headed inside to peel off our waterproof layers. I still just couldn't fathom accepting something like that.

As time went on and we got to know this one-legged fellow, we began to respect him as one of the most capable elders in the village. Accepting his halibut would not have been taking something away from him, as I had feared, rather it would have been honoring his ability to give something special to the teachers he was thankful for. I didn't allow him to bless us, and in so doing, I denied him the gift of giving. I don't think pity ever produces the right response.

But maybe something even uglier hid behind my pity. Maybe I didn't believe these people had anything to offer me. I was the giver; they were the recipients. I was here to rescue them.

The psychology world calls this a savior complex. We see a great need and we swoop down to meet said need. It starts as compassion and recognition of privilege, but those good things get twisted with pride and produce something more hurtful than helpful. The hero's "efforts to help others may be of an extreme nature that both deplete them ... and possibly enable the other individual."[1]

This complex is exacerbated every time we explain to people why we do what we do. We want our friends and family to understand the need so that our serving makes sense to them. We emphasize the struggles of the people we hope to reach, and we spout the statistics of how few of them are Christians. "See how much they need me?" we say.

Yes, we know they really need Jesus, not us; but as the bearers of His message, we tend to get ourselves mixed up with Him. And we forget how desperately we need Him, too. We forget that we can learn authentic love from the mentally handicapped, we can find deep fellowship with the open-hearted inmates, we can embrace true joy with the homeless and destitute, we can discover how to communicate on a heart level from the illiterate aboriginals, and we can receive gifts of gratitude with humility from those we came to serve.

How beautiful and sweet to recognize that we are all hurting humans in need of a savior, and how freeing to remember that you are not that savior.

I might have been a teacher by trade, but I needed to become a learner by heart.

Reflection Questions

When have you refused someone's offer because you felt sorry for them?

Do you recognize the "savior complex" anywhere in your own life?

Have you ever been enabled to continue unhealthy habits by someone else's charity?

It's Just Not a Good Time

SCHOOL STARTED THREE DAYS LATE because the water had been turned off while they were plumbing the bathrooms for the new gymnasium. I was incredibly relieved when we found out about the delayed start to the school year. It didn't feel like there was any way I could organize the disarray of my classroom and figure out the individual needs and education plan for each student, even if I had an entire extra month. Overwhelmed was an understatement.

On the first day of school, I had a rough plan in place for how to use multi-level grouping and centers to teach my seven diverse students; but this detailed standards based system, multi-grade classroom thing was a whole new can of worms for me. Grade levels were relatively inconsequential, only progress through the standards mattered; therefore, seven students times eight standard areas make forty-two unique subjects to prep. *Forty-two.*

Of course, younger students who progressed more quickly in, say, Math, could be grouped and taught simultaneously with slightly older students who struggled in Math. However, even figuring out how to group them accordingly was time-consuming. The cupboards full of resources left behind by the previous teacher were an organizational nightmare, so I spent an entire day just pulling everything out and sorting it in a way that seemed usable to me.

That first day, three of my seven students showed up. The rest were still on the fishing season schedule, traveling or on the boat with their families. This, alone, told me where education stood in life priorities here. The other students trickled in over the next few weeks, some eager and excited to meet me, others hesitant and reserved. Their sweet, round faces and thirst for attention drew me in. My heart wanted to connect, but I also felt the tension of being their teacher, their authority. How much could I give? How much should I hold back?

Since working hard in the classroom wasn't a value instilled in very many of them, I used all the motivational strategies I could think of and tried to stay on top of the standards I was required to teach; but I was nearly drowning under the load of it all.

The other new teachers weren't doing much better. We generally all looked like we had it together in the classroom on any given day, but it wasn't uncommon for Christine to come to me in tears of frustration about the attitudes of her middle-school boys who challenged her authority daily. And Jessica, well, we were starting to see a side of her that none of us could have expected.

Jessica had the additional, unique role of Head Teacher. Since our principal wasn't on site; she was technically in charge of all the staff at the school, responsible for keeping track of student attendance and payroll, and turning in the other monthly paperwork requirements. In other words, when the janitor didn't show up, she had the duty of finding a substitute or at least taking out the bathroom trash herself. We all recognized the intensity of this extra responsibility and wanted to help her out where we could, but she was very adamant about doing her job herself.

One morning, Troy arrived to dried mud on the floors and decided he would just give them a quick sweep before students arrived. When Jessica saw him, she exploded in anger. She interpreted it as him trying to steal her job, and she loathed him for it.

I went home that evening, email-vented to my mom, and decided to take my remaining frustration out on the stubborn rings of blue copper residue in my bathtub. Hard water—just another challenge of life in the bush. The fumes of the abrasive cleaner stung my eyes as I scrubbed at the mineral buildup. If only I could simply scrub away the buildup of difficulty in a few other areas of living here, as well. But, just like these rings, they would be back in time. Hard water, hard teaching, hard relationships. Just *hard*.

A knock sounded on the door. The pattering knock of a child, not the rhythmic knock of an adult.

Ugh, not now! I thought.

I stood up from my half-scrubbed tub and heaved a sigh of resignation. "Come in!"

Joy poked her head in the door. If ever there was a sweeter, cherub-cheeked face, I hadn't seen it. She brushed

COLLIDING WITH THE CALL

her straight black hair away from her smiling eyes. "Hi Mrs. Roberts! Can I visit?"

I should have been honored at this opportunity for relationship, this eight-year old's sincere desire to connect with me. Instead, I grumbled, "Uh, it's not really a good time. I'm cleaning my bathroom. Maybe a different day, okay?"

She nodded in understanding and closed the door. I watched out the window as she walked halfway down the boardwalk, then veered off to the playground where she sat swinging by herself.

Relieved at not having to endure her chatter, I returned to the bathroom. I just needed this time to clean, to be quiet. That's normal, right? Boundaries are good. I can't have students thinking they can just drop by, uninvited, whenever they want. Can I?

My shoulders slumped as I realized the disparity between this reality I was attempting to justify and my plans and hopes for being a place of refuge for our students. I rocked back on my heels and hung my head. I felt like a sham. I was not who I thought I would be here. I was like a water-saturated log, bobbing down the river with only one branch raised above the torrent. If even so much as a mosquito landed on that branch, the whole thing would submerge.

This was not what I had expected.

Oh, expectations. How often you have snatched the joy out of my life and created conflict in my relationships. I can't get away from you, for you crop up every time I visualize a change. I can't move forward without you right there, telling me what it might look like, feel like. Expectations are inescapable.

But they don't need to be inflexible. I've come to believe that expectations should not be thought of as *met* or *failed*. Rather, they are made to be *changed*. I entered life in Alaska expecting to be happy about my teaching, the way I was previously in a single-grade classroom with a team of supportive teachers around me, and instead I was frustrated. I should have adjusted my expectations, recognizing that this assignment would feel less fulfilling and more frustrating, and that's okay. I also expected to have enough emotional margin to offer relationship outside of the classroom to my students, and instead I was so tired I just wanted to hide. I should have altered my expectation to allow myself room to breathe without guilt.

I should have prayed for a new perspective on my situation and sought to see what God expected of me.

Let's talk for a moment about that idea of emotional margin and the guilt of not having any. Capacity for stress is a real thing; each person is different in how much stress they can handle and still maintain emotional and physical health. I might have known this as a fact, but I didn't offer myself any grace for discovering where the top line of my own capacity was drawn. I held myself to a high standard and felt intense guilt when I didn't reach that standard. Notice, this was not a standard God had set before me, this was my own creation. This was my idea of what a model missionary-teacher should look like.

Emotional margin means knowing yourself, accepting your limitations, and forgiving yourself for feeling maxed out. And it means seeking to make adjustments—to your daily habits, to your boundaries, and to your expectations—in order to revive your sense of well-being within your current situation. We are finite creatures. Limitations define us. But your limitations need not be your stumbling blocks; rather, your limitations can be your safety rails, guiding you along the path of rejoicing in your weaknesses where God can show His strength and grace (2 Cor. 12:10).

Knowing myself and accepting my limitations did not come easily in my early twenties. Twelve years later, it's still harder than I care to admit. But I'm learning. In that moment with Joy, God's grace would have been sufficient if I had simply invited her to hang out for a few minutes before returning to my cleaning, and God's grace would have been sufficient if I'd set the gentle boundary of asking my students to call before showing up. I did not need to expect myself to drop everything and play a board game with her for an hour every time she showed up, and I did not need to feel guilty for feeling overwhelmed in this early season of transitioning to teaching in the bush.

What I did need was an understanding at the soul level, of who God called me to be and what He was asking me to do. I needed to get my expectations in line with His.

Whenever I get angry over someone not meeting my expectations or feel shame over not meeting my own, this is where I need to go—to the feet of Jesus. In this very moment, this very situation, *who do You say that I am?* If He tells me my capacity is greater than I think it is, then I can stretch myself to give or forgive, knowing that His grace will meet me where I fall short. If He tells me to cease striving to be something I am not or forcing my standards on someone to be what they are not, then I can let go and rest, finding contentment and peace in our limitations. God is great. I don't need to be.

Reflection Questions

Think of a time you haven't met your own expectations. How did you respond?

We all have expectations, but they can always be changed. What specific expectations is God asking you to alter today?

Do you have emotional margin? What do you need to do to create it?

What Are You Even Doing Here?

ABOUT TWO MONTHS INTO THE school year, the district started talking about transferring one of us to teach in another village. The math was simple; our student count was down and theirs was up. Obviously, they wouldn't split Troy and me up, so it would either be Christine or Jessica. We fought to keep them both here, not wanting the upheaval that losing a teacher would bring to our classrooms and lives; but the district's responses were vague, and our balance felt delicate.

During this overwhelming, unpredictable season, we were invited to go to a church service in a nearby village; and we welcomed the opportunity to see a new place and worship with other believers. A travelling pastor picked us up in his four-seater airplane, and we hopped down the river to an even smaller village for church.

Before the service began, this well-intentioned pastor asked us if we'd met the only other Christian couple in our village. They were in their forties, had been following Christ for about four years, and had been praying for Christian teachers to fellowship with.

They didn't have any kids in the school, where our lives had been consumed with the task of adjusting to teaching; so no, we hadn't met them yet.

"Then what are you even doing here?" this short, fiery man retorted.

Somehow, I held it together in the moment, but I was absolutely pierced, soul deep. It was as if he'd said, "God put you there in answer to their prayers. You're in complete disobedience if you're not encouraging their faith!" I felt like a failure in this man's eyes, and even worse, I was afraid I was failing God. I struggled to really love my students with all their annoying habits and laziness, I couldn't get through to Jessica's heart, and I had honestly no motivation to reach out to this other Christian couple. What *was* I even doing there?

I tried to sit through the worship, but the pain inside was too strong. I got up, closed myself in the small bathroom, and tried to stifle my sobs.

Is THIS your plan, God? This mess of a job I'm calling teaching? This dreadful up and down chaos of Jessica's emotions? This crushing expectation of supporting the other Christian couple? Seriously, God. I don't like it. I can't do it. Why am I even here?

I knew I needed to pull it together, but I had no answer. No peace. Only pain. Some missionary I was.

It wasn't long after that when the storm came, and it rained and rained for days until the lake overflowed her shores and the beach in front of our house disappeared under the muddy waters. The murk rose into the crawl space of our duplex, pausing mere inches below our floor.

It was an apt picture of my heart, flooded with swirling confusion and feelings of failure that threatened to make a mess of everything. At that point I claimed every storm

WHAT ARE YOU EVEN DOING HERE?

analogy in the Bible and in music. I tried to remind myself that Jesus was there with me, even though I couldn't see him through the crashing waves. But honestly, it just hurt. And I wanted out.

Thus began my breaking. My undoing. The long, dark night of my soul.

God had parted the sea to get us here, but now I was in the wilderness with the Israelites, looking back over my shoulder and longing for Egypt. I was homesick and weary and hungry. This couldn't be what God intended when He invited me to follow Him. He promised milk and honey, but instead, "My tears have been my food day and night" (Psalm 42:3).

But I forgot about the waiting. The Israelites wandered in the desert for forty years. The Church has been watching for Jesus' "imminent" return for over 2,000 years. While we wait, while we wander, while we watch, God is at work.

It's here, in the wilderness, that we are taken apart, piece by piece, by the Master Craftsman who has a much greater design in mind. There is no magic carpet to fly us from Egypt to the Promised Land. We must walk through the wilderness, step by step, to get there.

When has someone you respected said or done something harsh that really crushed you?

Describe how God has allowed certain seasons of your life to feel completely overwhelming.

How has your faith weathered those storms?

A Piece of Pie

IT WAS NOVEMBER. WE WERE in somewhat of a groove with school, feeling like we were starting to grasp the system and really meet our students' needs. We had finally met the other Christian couple and doing a weekly Bible study with Benny and Kim had become a mutual blessing. They were incredibly generous people with an unrivaled love for Jesus. We were, in fact, thankful for the kick in the pants we had received that got us moving toward a relationship with them.

It was almost Thanksgiving, and since holidays are always hard away from family, all of us teachers decided that we would gather and make it a special celebration. Jessica insisted on preparing the entire meal—something she did for her family back home that would help her feel like she was maintaining her traditions. I talked her into letting me contribute a pie, and we planned to host the meal at our apartment.

Christine decided to invite one of her students and his single dad, which we thought was a great idea; so there would be seven of us total. We carried Stanley's table and chairs into our apartment and set up for the feast. I rolled out pie crust and tried to get in the holiday mood with some Christmas music. We were making the most of this isolated situation, and it was beginning to feel like maybe we'd be okay after all.

73

A knock on the door interrupted my baking, and I hollered for the visitor to come in. Christine entered, looking confused and a bit frustrated.

"Jessica says she isn't going to come today," she burst out.

"What?! Why?" I asked.

She rolled her eyes. "Who knows? But she said she'll still make the food."

Sadly, this was typical for Jessica; but I honestly didn't expect it on Thanksgiving, which she said was her favorite holiday of the entire year. I decided to try to talk to her, but it was no use. Her mind was made up.

Dinner time rolled around, Stanley came over, the student and his dad came over, and finally Jessica started bringing over the food. I helped her carry the remaining side dishes and tried once more to invite her to join us, even for just a few minutes; but she wouldn't have anything to do with it—with *us*—that day.

I remember trying to make light of it and just enjoy the meal, but it was incredibly awkward. To top it all off, my pie crust was rock hard. As in, it had to be sawn through with a knife. Some things just can't be salvaged.

It was shortly after that when we learned that Jessica had requested to be transferred to the other village that needed a teacher. We had only a couple of short weeks to figure out how we would split up her class load and Head Teacher duties. In the end, Troy took all the subjects for 7 - 12th grade, and I became the Head Teacher since I was good at paperwork. Once again, we were swamped and overwhelmed.

All I wanted was a nice piece of pie I could actually bite through.

The day Jessica flew out, Troy walked into his classroom to find a letter on his desk. In it, she vehemently spewed her feelings toward him. She cut down his methods as a teacher and insisted that he was impossible to work with. She also reiterated how strongly she loathed the fact that we were Christians, believing in an ill-intentioned god. Troy is pretty good at shaking off emotional attacks, but after trying so hard to work peacefully alongside her and helping her in so many ways, this final blow left its mark.

I wasn't loving the paperwork as Head Teacher, but I was figuring it out. Timesheets, maintenance requests, attendance logs, book and supply inventories. All that was straightforward. It was managing the people that stole my peace time and time again. Hunting school employees down to collect their timesheets was annoying. Finding last-minute subs when the janitor, or the cook, or the P.E. aide, or the secretary didn't show up was difficult. But putting on the tough face of a boss over people twice my age? That was well beyond my character or my experience. I teach young children—children you can pick up and move if they are endangering someone, children who give you their attention if you ring a bell or flick the lights. Culturally different adults who have worked at the school for ten or more years? You might as well ask me to lasso a moose.

75

My classroom aide was a sweet, small lady whose son was in Christine's class. She wasn't great at managing student behavior, but she was a willing helper when I had the kids rotate through stations or needed a snack prepared. One day, early in the school year, she invited all the teachers to her house for her son's birthday. We quickly learned that this was how all birthdays were celebrated, with a large spread of food provided by the family and most of the village invited to partake in the feast.

At this birthday party, my aide and a couple of her friends stepped outside for a few minutes. When they came back in, she smelled like smoke. I didn't think anything of it. We were in her home, after all, and it's perfectly legal for an adult to use cigarettes. My aide felt the need to apologize, though. She told me that she was embarrassed and hadn't wanted me to know that she smoked. This was a disturbing glimpse into the pedestal that teachers are put on, and the shame the villagers feel over their habits that they know are taught against in the school.

Several months later, under my watch as Head Teacher, I began to suspect that my aide was hiding something worse from me at school. Her attendance had become more sporadic, and her breath smelled suspiciously like alcohol. I'm pretty inexperienced with these things, so I didn't push the issue until the day one of my students came to me in private and said, "Aunty has vodka in her water bottle." She clearly wasn't as naive as I was.

I squirmed. I didn't want to confront her, but I needed confirmation, so I gave her a copy job to do and took a quick sniff of her bottle. It was *not* water. I called the principal, who was scheduled to visit our school soon anyway, and together we did the agonizing job of firing her. Now I had a broken relationship, no aide, and one more crack in my hopes of surviving this gig.

Perhaps equally challenging was the day our secretary called in sick for work, then came in the next week with half of her face black and blue. Our principal had warned us about this. He'd seen it before with her, and we had instructions to talk to her right away about the possibility of domestic violence. She flat out denied it. But her sister, our cook who liked to gossip, told us another story. I so badly wanted to help this gentle, hard-working woman; but she wasn't about to turn her husband in. And why would she? She didn't want to leave him. Where would she go in a tiny village? She didn't want him to go to jail and have to deal with court proceedings. She just wanted to cover over the pain and keep on surviving.

So did everyone else. Making the hard change or dealing with the guilt was simply too much. I think I'll rename this place, Unresolved Grief.

Grief happens when you are separated from someone or something you are attached to. It's often viewed as a process that you move through in stages; however, the journey might be more of a looping roller coaster than a straight path. And that's okay—everyone grieves differently. The trouble comes when you get stuck in a stage, such as anger or depression, and can never move forward to acceptance of the loss.

Before moving to Alaska, I read a book called *The Grieving Indian*.[1] Through this moving story, I discovered that grief can occur on a community level, as well. As a very broad and obvious example, the Jews share their grief over the Holocaust. And many indigenous people groups carry grief over a loss of land and freedom that is generations deep. In addition to this reality in our village, most individuals had tragically lost a loved one. Plenty of people were hurting, and substance abuse was a common coping mechanism.

What I didn't recognize, however, was that I was grieving, too. I had lost both my normal and my dream. I didn't just *miss* the church we left behind, I was *grieving* the loss of it. Our family lived in Idaho and we knew we would return there for visits, not to Minnesota where we lived temporarily during college and the first two years of teaching. Everything I missed about Minnesota was a complete loss, and I grieved it. That place of normal was dead and gone. And my dream to serve joyfully through teaching as missions felt dead, too. This very emotional journal entry made after we returned from Christmas break that year captures the stage of depression I was in:

I've found myself crying uncontrollably since returning.

Right now, I just really hope and pray this is only for a season. This is such a miserable place to live. We spend most of our waking hours in the school, teaching or preparing to teach students who, for the most part, have no interest in what we have to say.

When we bumped and swerved our way to a landing yesterday, we stepped off the plane to a wind chill of - 38 degrees Fahrenheit. We don't have hardly any water pressure today, and I'm dreading spending my Sunday afternoon at the school.

I had no idea that this was a typical, albeit painful, part of the grieving process. And while nobody wants to grieve, we all will while living on this planet. We'll shed our tears and fight our battles and hold hands with those who cry and fight, as well. Know that you have permission to grieve. Even if your loss seems insignificant compared to someone else's, it is as real and powerful as it feels to you. Don't get stuck in denying it or being angry about it. Feel it. Feel it all. You're not weak or broken for feeling grief. I wish someone had told me that then, so I'm telling you now.

If we invite God, our Healer and Redeemer, into the process of grief, we have the ultimate assurance that we will come out on the other side to more than just acceptance—to hope. And remember hope produced through suffering? It will not disappoint us. It will lead us to the arms of our Father who will wipe away every tear from our eyes when He brings His perfect *shalom* one day. His *shalom,* His peace, passes all understanding. It brings wholeness, satisfaction, and restoration. We do not grieve as those who have no hope (1 Thessalonians 4:13), we grieve as those who are watching for the return of their resurrected King.

We have resurrection hope. But before anything can be resurrected, it must die.

Reflection Questions

What have you lost (home, job, loved one, dreams, security, community, etc.) that you have grieved?

Ask the Lord to reveal any places you might be "stuck," covering over the pain rather than learning to live with it.

Consider this thought:
"We do not grieve as those who have no hope (1 Thess. 4:13), we grieve as those who are watching for the return of their resurrected King.

We have resurrection hope. But before anything can be res-urrected, it must die."

How does this make you feel?

Walking on Water

WINTER RESTED FROM HER USUALLY gusting fury, and the frozen lake crackled under the stillness. Snow pants, heavy boots, down jacket, faux-fur lined hat with ear flaps tied under my chin, waterproof mittens—my armored suit against the chill. My footsteps crunched through the drifts on the beach and I stepped out onto the ice. Thick, grey ice decorated with white bubbles and deep fissures.

Cold air bit my nose as I walked farther out onto the expanse of water. White lake, white shores, white mountains, white clouds tipped in gold and pink from the sun's reach from the horizon. I breathed in the frozen silence and trekked onward. Toward the mountains, toward the sky, deeper into the peace.

Face turned upward, a crystalline angel spread her cloud wings over me. Or maybe a hovering dove. The presence of God here. With me. Above me in the breadth of the shimmering sky. Below me in the mysterious ice. Next to me, walking on the water. Watching over this village, yearning for her trust, her worship, her healing.

The hum of a small engine cut through my reverie, and a remote-control airplane swooped in front of my cloud angel. I watched it dip and land and take off again. Rounding a peninsula, I saw one of the 5th grade boys with the controller. When he saw me, he landed his plane in front of me and ran over. Excitement brimmed between us as he showed me his Christmas gift. We smiled and laughed, and as he walked back toward the shore, I found the peace that much sweeter now that it had been touched by a child.

God was in this place, and that was making a difference. God's presence is what makes all the difference. Like the pillar of cloud by day and fire by night that led the Israelites through the desert, God would lead me through my wilderness, too.

Most days I felt like Moses, uncertain about the future and crying out, "If your Presence does not go with us, do not send us up from here," but there were those precious moments when I was still enough to hear His promise, "My Presence will go with you, and I will give you rest" (Exodus 33:14-15).

The very Presence of Yahweh—the great I AM—is both an unfathomably beautiful and terrifying place. Moses spoke with God in the burning bush, in the pillar of cloud, and in the storm on top of Mount Sinai. He was intimate with God as with a friend, and even his very face radiated the glory of God after speaking with Him in the tabernacle. But that glory faded, and while Moses heard the voice of God and experienced various representations of His presence, Moses still wanted more.

Every glimpse of the Almighty leaves us longing for more. Deep within our spirits, we know that our Creator is the source of all goodness, all fullness, all joy, all beauty, all righteousness, all wisdom, all love, all *life*. A taste of the richness of His Presence stirs an insatiable hunger for more. Perhaps this is why Moses, even after all his "face to face" conversations with the Lord, still begged to see God's glory. It was as if he was saying, "Lord! Stop hiding from me! I don't want a cloud, I want You. I can't do what You're asking me to do if You're not with me, and I need to see You to seal the deal."

God couldn't grant Moses his full request, because no man can see the Lord and live, but He did reveal the backside of His glory as He hid Moses in a rock and allowed him to see the train of His robe. His goodness, His mercy, His compassion, His grace, His faithfulness, His patience, His love, and His justice trailed behind Him. And yet, I bet that even after that unprecedented display of God's glory, Moses still craved more. The more that comes only through Jesus.

"The Word became flesh and made his dwelling among us. We have seen his glory, the glory of the one and only Son, who came from the Father, full of grace and truth... For the law was given through Moses; grace and truth came through Jesus Christ. No one has ever seen God, but the one and only Son, who is himself God and is in closest relationship with the Father, has made him known."
JOHN 1:14,17-18

85

In that wilderness place, where it felt like everything I loved was dying and even the revelation of God seemed small compared to the task, I could choose to remind my hungry soul that when God sent Jesus, He did indeed seal the deal. He showed me His fullness, and He promised that He would never leave me nor forsake me. Even when I couldn't see Him, or feel His presence, or hear His voice, I could cling to the truth. In the dark night, Jesus would be enough.

As a special end of the year event, we took the entire school on a four-hour hike to the mouth of the river that empties into the lake. We took the precautions of enlisting parents to be front and rear guards with guns as bear protection, and we brought a four-wheeler along for the student with cerebral palsy, but the rest of us navigated the trail by foot and were rewarded at the end with a beautiful black sand beach for our picnic. I stored in my heart those precious moments of holding my students' hands to help them down slippery hills, and of laughing freely with the parent volunteers, feeling almost like we were accepted as friends—more little reminders of God's presence with me.

We had done it. We had survived our first year, the upheaval of Jessica leaving, and the searing journey into the raw places of our souls that happens when trials are faced. Our contract was signed to return the following year, as was Christine's, and we left for the summer with hopes that having this first difficult year under our belts would make the next one easier.

Reflection Questions

Describe a time that the awareness of God's presence comforted you.

Meditate on Exodus 33. What is God saying to you through this passage?

Part 3

THE LINGERING NIGHT

"Lord, my God, who am I that You should forsake me?
The Child of your Love—and now become as the most
hated one—the one—You have thrown away as un-
wanted—unloved. I call, I cling, I want—and there is
no One to answer—no One on Whom I can cling—no,
No One. Alone ... Where is my Faith—even deep down
right in there is nothing, but emptiness & darkness—
My God—how painful is this unknown pain—I have no
Faith—I dare not utter the words and thoughts that
crowd in my heart and make me suffer untold agony."

— Mother Teresa, AN UNDATED LETTER TO JESUS[1]

Going Back for More

WE SPENT OUR SUMMER WITH family, soaking up the comforts of home, and relishing the weekly services at the little country church I had grown up in. Shortly before returning to Alaska, I was asked to sing a special number at church for our send-off service, so the pianist and I chose "I'll Go Where You Want Me to Go,"[1] an old hymn that I had sung in a church choir a couple of years prior. She and I reminisced a bit about her daughter, who had suddenly died several months before while serving in missions overseas, and of the challenges and rewards of obedience. The lyrics were all too fitting:

> *I'll go where you want me to go, dear Lord, o'er mountain, or plain, or sea.*
> *I'll say what you want me to say, dear Lord; I'll be what you want me to be.*

Yes, this was the longing of my heart—to serve the Lord without reservation, without excuse, with total abandon. But as I stood in front of that tiny church and attempted to sing my conviction, a sob choked my voice before I could finish the chorus. Tears dripped off my chin as the memories of the pain of obedience, the fear for what we were about to return to, and the embarrassment over losing it in front of a crowd flowed over me. The gracious pianist took

91

up the singing for me until I could pull together a squeaky-voiced finish.

When the song ended, she joined me on the stage, wrapped her arm around my shoulder, and gently explained to the congregation the rawness this song evoked in the memory of her daughter's recent passing. Oh, if she only knew the real reason I wept. But no one outside of my immediate family and Troy really knew. How could they? I could hardly explain it, nor did I want to relive it in order to share it. So I kept up the appearance of the good soldier returning to her post.

We flew to Anchorage and stayed in our mission guest house while we boxed up cartloads of groceries from Costco and Fred Meyer. That old guest house smelled of musty wood and love. When we were there, we were reminded that we were part of a big family, all facing the same kinds of challenges, all praying for God to bring healing and hope to the spiritually dark villages we worked in. I wished I could bring that smell with me.

We packed our crate of eggs in a Rubbermaid tote between rolls of paper towels, took cereal bags out of their boxes to make more space, carefully weighed each tote to make sure it was under 50 pounds, and took our six months' worth of groceries to the post office. Hopefully those eggs wouldn't freeze and crack in the belly of the airplane. Hopefully the bags of flour wouldn't explode (again). Hopefully the toilet paper rolls wouldn't get too terribly smashed.

With wheeled coolers full of meat and produce, we checked in for the first leg of our journey back to the bush. I stared at the tarmac out the window, feeling both filled and empty at the same time. The summer break had restored some life to my weary soul, but looking at the year ahead made me wonder if I had anything substantial to offer those hurting kids in my classroom.

Just ahead of us, a dog sat with its owner. It looked part husky and seemed content to rest by its master's feet. Then the call came to board, and the dog's owner commanded it into its kennel. It hesitated. The owner tugged its collar and commanded more sternly, and the dog obeyed, tail between its legs. As I watched that dog cower in its kennel, it was as if I was looking in the mirror.

That was me. I felt like God was saying, "Go!" and I didn't want to go. I'd made the choice long ago to follow Him, to obey him, to serve Him, and I knew in my head that He knew what was best for me, but I felt trapped. I felt like He was shoving me in a kennel, about to launch me back into the place of my fears.

But maybe that's what it was all about. Maybe serving God wasn't "the only place I'd ever be happy," as I had somehow absorbed growing up. Maybe God was more of an army commander, and I was a disposable soldier.

After all, how many characters in the Bible had it easy or pleasant after receiving a call from God? Abraham? Commanded to leave his home country and had to wait for what seemed like ages for a promised son. Joseph? Sold

COLLIDING WITH THE CALL

into slavery and put in prison in order to accomplish God's will of ensuring provision for his family. Moses? Commanded to return to the land he was a fugitive from and confront the most powerful man in the world with only a miraculous stick. The prophets? Basically ignored and abused for sharing God's word. And have you heard of all the brutal ways the apostles were put to death for proclaiming the message of Christ? Seriously, I don't want to be swallowed by a fish or something, so, "Yes, Sir, I'll obey you!"

My theology was swinging like a pendulum, but it was the only way I could reconcile what was happening in my life with my faith.

It seems we humans are good at seeing whichever side of our multifaceted God we want to see. Our finite minds cannot comprehend the fullness of an infinite God, so He graciously reveals Himself to us in numerous stories and pictures and words that we can understand. I love this about Him. I can stare at an oak tree and receive multiple revelations about both my Creator and myself:

The wise Creator gives the tree deep roots to ensure it won't fall over and to nourish it as it draws water and nutrients from deep in the earth, even when rain is scarce.

The detailed Creator designed symmetrical leaves filled with verdant, sun-absorbing chlorophyll that don shades of yellow, orange, and red when painted by frost's icy hand.

The nurturing Creator spreads the oak's branches wide, providing a home for the birds, food for the squirrels, and shade for the weary passerby.

The patient Creator ordained the tree to grow in seasons, from the acorn lying dormant under the snow to the blossoming growth of Spring to the fruitful produce of Summer to the sorrowful glory of Fall to the barrenness of Winter that waits again for the Spring.

If I am that tree, then in that season I believe I was the acorn. I felt detached from all that once gave me life and security, unaware that the potential inside me would never grow if I had stayed on the tree. I felt crushed under the weight of the snow, not realizing that it pushed me deeper into the soil where I could sprout, unharmed. I felt frozen in Winter's stillness, unable to see through the darkness that surrounded me to the Spring that would surely come. And I saw the Creator as the cruel hand that plucked me from my branch and flung me aside, not knowing the tender care with which He had placed me into the snow and now stood watching over me.

It's difficult to see past our circumstances and through our pain. This is why we need stories to illuminate our path through the darkness. I mentioned Joseph earlier; if ever there lived an example of coming out victorious on the other side of a deep pit, it's him.

Genesis 37 and 39 through 45 detail the ups and downs of his life. When Joseph is probably just a teenager, favored by his father and excited about life, God reveals his future as a great ruler to him in his dreams. Honestly, I find this timing odd. What did it accomplish, besides stir Joseph's pride and his brothers' contempt, to allow him to know that his family would one day bow down to him? I imagine this prophetic dream brought Joseph comfort in the hard times, but also despair when it felt like it would never happen. Nonetheless, God gave it to him and set His plan in motion.

A plan that would take Joseph to the bottom of a cistern at his brothers' hands and into servitude in Egypt. Imagine him, the child who was once given whatever he wanted, bound and sold as a utilitarian item. Could it get any bleaker? A rich man named Potiphar buys him, and Joseph has to acquire a new language and the ways of a common slave. But he learns quickly, and it seems like everything he touches is blessed; so, Potiphar puts him in charge of his household. Yes! The upswing. Maybe Joseph will continue to be promoted and he can return to his family a wealthy, free man one day.

But then his good looks get him in trouble. Potiphar's wife wants him, and when he refuses her enticements time after time, she finally snaps. "He tried to take advantage of me!" she wails, the temptress playing the victim. So, Joseph is dumped into the dungeon. Another pit. Wasn't he just in one of these? But again, God's presence gives Joseph favor with the chief guard and he is put in charge of the other prisoners.

One day, after who knows how long, Pharaoh's cupbearer and baker are thrown into jail, too. They have dreams, Joseph interprets them, and he asks the cupbearer to remember him when he is restored to his position. "The chief cupbearer, however, did not remember Joseph; he forgot him" (Genesis 40:23). Ouch. Hopes dashed—again. Two more years go by before Pharaoh has a dream and the cupbearer finally remembers Joseph.

Joseph is cleaned up, made presentable for the King of Egypt after his years in confinement, and he has a chance to interpret Pharaoh's dream. This next part is probably my favorite scene from the whole story: Joseph is standing in the palace, opulence surrounding him, the scent of freedom in the air (which surely smelled heaps better than a dank prison), and when Pharaoh says, "I've heard it said of you that when you hear a dream you can interpret it," Joseph replies, "Actually, I can't." Seriously? Pharaoh could have thrown him right back where he came from at that remark without hearing the rest. But Joseph, wisened and patient from his trials, makes sure to give God credit. "But God will give Pharaoh the answer he desires."

Indeed, God does. He shows Pharaoh that the land would have seven years of plenty followed by seven years of a severe famine. Then Joseph casually suggests a plan: put a discerning man in charge of Egypt to store up food during the fruitful years so the country won't be ruined by the famine. Yes, good idea. So, Pharaoh raises Joseph to his second in command. At that point, Joseph is thirty. I find it intriguing that the Bible includes his age here. It's the biblical age for beginning priestly service, and it's also

97

the age at which Jesus began his ministry. But it also hints at the number of years that he has already been separated from his family—possibly even half of his life. But God's plan was just starting to unfold.

Joseph is then given a wife and they have two sons. He names the first one Manasseh, because he forgot the troubles of his youth, and the second one is called Ephraim, because God made him fruitful in the land of his suffering. The years he spent in the pit of suffering were being redeemed, and he wanted to remember God's goodness to him every time he called his sons by name.

I'm sure you know the rest of the story, how Joseph's brothers eventually come to buy grain, how Joseph tests their sincerity, and how they are eventually reconciled to each other. Then Joseph says this: "And now, do not be distressed and do not be angry with yourselves for selling me here, because it was to save lives that God sent me ahead of you" (Genesis 45:5). Through this wild, twisted series of events, God preserves His chosen family and so many more. Finally, even Joseph's father, Jacob—the one God renamed Israel—at 130 years young, joins them in Egypt where they multiply and prosper.

We read the end of the story, and we nod. It's good. God's plan is good… as long as I'm not Joseph in the bottom of the pit.

But when you *do* find yourself in that bleak place where God's promises and your dreams seem nigh impossible, remember Joseph. Remember the end. Remember the God whose hand has been writing your story from the beginning and know that it is good.

He is good.

Reflection Questions

Does the longing "to serve the Lord without reservation, without excuse, with total abandon" resonate with you? Does it frighten you?

Have you ever felt trapped in the call of God or like His will for your life was a prison?

What facet of God's character is most prominent in your thinking right now?

Beyond Survival

JUST A COUPLE OF WEEKS into this new school year, we got a call from our regional team leader. He knew some of the struggles of our first year and recognized the need for us to be intentional in our overall health, so he wisely asked me, "What are you doing this year, beyond just surviving?"

I knew what he meant. I knew why he asked. And I had no answer for him. *I came back. I'm doing the best I can to tread water. Isn't that all anyone can do in the midst of constantly crashing waves?* His query struck a chord deep within me, and I realized that I wanted to thrive. I wanted that abundant life Jesus promises. I wanted to be content in the calling and not kick back at God. I wanted a richer experience than just surviving, but I was clueless about how to get there. I began to doubt if what I wanted was even possible in this particular place.

Meanwhile, Benny and Kim, the only resident Christians in the village, were also feeling the need to step out of the struggles for a bit of a reprieve spiritually, so they planned to stay the winter in a bigger town. Before they left, however, they wanted to host a special retreat at their fishing lodge across the lake. They invited the fiery pastor who had rebuked us a year ago, our team leader, and a handful of other Christians from the neighboring villages.

The retreat was a sweet two days of fellowship, studying the Word together, and praying for one another. But it also symbolized to me all that we were missing in our daily life and the loss we were about to experience when Benny and Kim moved. I remember struggling through much of that time, trying to smile, and avoiding going too deep in answer to people's friendly questions.

"God, how do I get beyond just surviving?" my soul cried out.

Their beautiful fishing lodge was the only building on the far side of the lake and its large bay windows gazed across to the other shore where our duplex, the school, and a world of hurting people and problems huddled together. I stared over the gray waters at that life that seemed miles away and still somehow gripped my heart in its stranglehold. I wasn't in a healthy place spiritually or emotionally and I knew it. Something had to give before I did.

Somewhere in that time frame, a short piece of classical Christian literature found its way into my hands. I have no recollection of where it came from, but Hannah Whitall Smith's book, *The Christian's Secret to a Happy Life*, was what God gave me for that season.

Early in the book she says, "But notwithstanding all your knowledge and all your activities in the service of the Lord, your souls are secretly starving, and you cry out again and again for that bread and water of life which you saw promised in the Scriptures to all believers."[1] *Um, yes! How did you know?*

In chapter 8, she starts out with a long compilation of verses reminding the reader of God's sovereignty over every little thing, His strength, and the promises of His presence in the life of the believer. Then she goes on to describe the key to abiding in the perfect peace of Christ.

"To my own mind, these Scriptures, and many others like them, settle forever the question as to the power of second causes in the life of the children of God. They are all under the control of our Father, and nothing can touch us, except by His knowledge and with His permission. It may be the sin of man that originates the action, and therefore the thing itself cannot be said to be the will of God but by the time it reaches us, it has become God's will for us, and must be accepted as directly from His hands. No man or company of men, no power in earth or heaven, can touch that soul which is abiding in Christ, without first passing through Him, and receiving the seal of His permission. If God be for us, it matters not who may be against us; nothing can disturb or harm us, except He shall see that it is best for us, and shall stand aside to let it pass."[2]

She also offered the image of the presence of God surrounding us like a bubble of impenetrable light, a shield on every side. Nothing passes through His protective presence without His wise and loving permission. *Nothing passes through His protective presence without His wise and loving permission.* Could I really believe that? I realized that I had been picturing myself as separate from God—I was floundering under the waves; Jesus was walking on top of them. I could only catch glimpses of him, and it felt as if my hand kept slipping out of his grasp. But to see myself as constantly surrounded by the protective presence of my loving Father gave me a completely different perspective on the storm. He was my life raft.

Soon enough we were climbing into an airplane to spend Fall in-service in the "big village." We began to develop closer relationships with the other teachers from our district, we bought milk and ice cream and cheese for unbelievably high prices at the store, and we spent the evenings with our small but growing regional team. This year we met with not only our team leader's family, but also with another young family who had joined them and one other teaching couple. These precious people became like family to us, and we always looked forward to the school breaks we would get to spend with them.

God was providing the relationships we craved. He was realigning my beliefs to His truth. And I began to trust that He was truly with me in the chaos. The hero facade that I had worn as we walked into our village over a year ago had been stripped away, and I was learning to be thankful for that.

There were some practical changes that needed to happen too; so as much as I hated admitting my weakness, Troy and I decided that he would take over the official Head Teacher position at the start of the second semester, even though I would still help him with a lot of the paperwork. I still wasn't sure what thriving looked like, but it felt like survival might not be quite so painful anymore.

The temptation for those of us who like to think of ourselves as servants is that we tend to think this idea of serving extends only to others, not ourselves. We pour our time and energy into the people and activities we feel responsible for. We take Philippians 2:3-4 seriously:

"Do nothing out of selfish ambition or vain conceit. Rather, in humility value others above yourselves, not looking to your own interests but each of you to the interests of others."

But I think some misinterpretation of this verse creeps in, or at least it did for me. I believed that it meant care for others should always usurp care for myself. But is this true? Let's look at the following verses, 5-8:

"In your relationships with one another, have the same mindset as Christ Jesus: Who, being in very nature God, did not consider equality with God something to be used to his own advantage; rather, he made himself nothing by taking the very nature of a servant, being made in human likeness. And being found in appearance as a man, he humbled himself by becoming obedient to death—even death on a cross!"

105

What I see here is a call to Christlike humility and love that lays down its life for its friends. That's a lofty aspiration. One I have come to learn that I can't grab hold of on my own. In fact, the harder I try, the wearier I become and the more difficult it is to value others above myself. If my own soul is parched, I can't expect to have any overflow for those around me.

I didn't understand this during our time in Alaska, but what I can now tell myself in hindsight is that the missing key to a life that thrives is soul care. I cannot display the mind of Christ without being filled with the Spirit, and I cannot be filled with the Spirit if I'm running in circles, desperately trying to look out for the interests of others.

Backing up to verse 1 in Philippians 2, we find the recipe for the servant-hearted humility we long for. "Therefore if you have any encouragement from being united with Christ, if any comfort from his love, if any common sharing in the Spirit..." I must make time and space in my life and heart to be united with Christ, comforted by His love, and enfolded in the Spirit. Then his mindset of placing others' interests above my own will naturally, without artificial effort, become my mindset.

At that point in my life, my soul care amounted to reading a chapter of the Bible with breakfast, praying before bed, reading Christian books, and occasionally taking a peaceful walk. Oh, and creative writing. I didn't recognize that as a place of connecting with God, but it certainly was and still is. Not bad, but definitely not enough for the intensity of the laying down of my life that teaching in the bush required. Even in these activities I recognize a doing, a striving, a rushing. Coming out of Bible classes in college, I had learned to engage on a deeply intellectual level with Scripture. I'd lost the art of sitting with it and letting Him speak it over me and right through me. My prayers were intentional and structured, making sure I mentioned all my loved ones at least once a week. I hadn't learned how to ask the Lord questions and listen for the answers. My reading, walking, and writing were usually done to escape. I didn't know how to invite Jesus into those times and receive the comfort of His love.

Yes, there was much to come before I would feel I was really thriving, not just surviving, but God kept me afloat on the life raft of His presence; and before we knew it, it was time to sign our contracts for our third year of teaching. And with just the faintest bit more confidence than the previous year, we did.

Reflection Questions

Right now, in this moment, what are you doing beyond just surviving?

Do you believe that *"nothing passes through His protective presence without His wise and loving permission"*? Why or why not?

Do you tend to picture Jesus as separate from you, like you're trying to reach out for him, or surrounding you, like a life raft in the storm?

What does soul care look like for you right now?

Desperate for Peace

LOOKING OUT THE SMALL AIRPLANE window at our village nestled among the lush August foliage, I smiled, recognizing a small sense of homecoming that had never been there before. After landing, we were greeted warmly, and although I had no idea what this year would bring, I was thankful for the peace that passes all understanding that I could feel guarding my heart. I would need to draw strength from it sooner than I could have imagined.

That night, we were awakened around 1:00 AM by loud knocking on our door. Troy answered, I could hear the upset voice of one of the village men, the door closed, and the lock clicked, and Troy returned with disturbing news.

A party had gotten out of control, a fight had broken out, and one young man had just killed another young man with an axe. He was hiding somewhere in the bushes, the State Troopers would arrive in the morning, and we were instructed to keep our door locked and not offer asylum if the murderer came around.

This is insane, I thought. *This* place *is insane! God, I can't believe what just happened.*

And yet, as I sat there, shocked, I again felt God's peace. My mind started scrolling through the families involved, and I knew they would be beside themselves with grief and uncertainty. Troy and I prayed for them, and I was thankful we were there to pray. Who else was there to ask God to

109

give them comfort, to reveal Himself to them amid the pain?

In the morning, the young man turned himself in without a struggle; and strangely, village life carried on as normal. School started a few days later, and I gave extra space for grieving to my student who had just lost her big brother. She was irritable and emotional for a while, but it seemed as though grief and tragedy were already such common themes here, that it really didn't change anything all that much.

But buried pain only grows until it can't be hidden anymore.

About three months later, we woke up at 4:00 AM to the sound of yelling. We looked out our window and could see flames coming from what appeared to be the far side of the school. Thinking the gym was on fire, we threw on our boots and coats and ran outside.

It didn't take us long to realize that the flames weren't coming from the school but from the abandoned house next to it. The house where the murder had taken place.

Half of the village was there, watching the show. Men were prepared to keep the fire from spreading, but no one was trying to put it out. I looked around at the faces near me. Lit by orange, flickering light, most were solemn, and a few were tear stained. This wasn't arson so much as it was catharsis. An attempt to purge the soul of its pain by removing the source of the reminder. An attempt to find peace by releasing the internal chaos.

But while we need those times of unreservedly expressing our feelings, peace won't be found in the emptiness that follows the emotional outpour. Peace has only one source. Peace has a name.

Jesus.

Watching that vengeful fire burn, seeing it consume the house the way I knew it would consume their hearts, I desperately wanted to introduce these mourners to the Fountain of Peace. I wanted to show them the path of hope and healing. But there were walls—so many walls. We hadn't yet earned the right to teach them about anything beyond math and reading.

So, we went back home and attempted to sleep for two or so hours before the school day began. Instead, I lay awake, staring into the darkness and asking myself if I really knew anything about peace.

Most of the past two years I had spent my days feeling frustrated, helpless, discouraged, or overwhelmed. Anything but peaceful. But then there was that reminder again: Peace is a person.

"He himself is our peace," claims Ephesians 2:14, and, "he will be called ... Prince of Peace," says Isaiah 9:6.

I did know Peace. And because I knew Him, I could, even in the most tumultuous circumstances, sense His peace, feel His peace, trust His peace.

Philippians 4:6-7 has long been one of my favorite memory verses: "Do not be anxious about anything, but in every situation, by prayer and petition, with thanksgiving, present your requests to God. And the peace of God, which transcends all understanding, will guard your hearts and your minds in Christ Jesus."

The peace of God transcends all understanding. In other words, it doesn't make any sense. It can't be figured out or reasoned into. When we pray, and especially when we give thanks, He lavishes it on us. It's a gift of grace. In fact, Paul's favorite greeting was "grace and peace to you," (Romans 1:7, 1 Corinthians 1:3, Galatians 1:3, and just about every other letter he wrote). And he speaks often of peace elsewhere in his epistles: "For the kingdom of God is not a matter of eating and drinking, but of righteousness, peace and joy in the Holy Spirit," (Romans 14:17), "May the God of hope fill you with all joy and peace as you trust in him," (Romans 15:13), and "Now may the Lord of peace himself give you peace at all times and in every way," (2 Thessalonians 3:16).

Just notice the words that peace is paired with: grace, righteousness, joy, and hope. And just like grace, righteousness, joy, and hope, we can't contrive peace on our own. We receive peace when we receive Him. We have peace because we have Him. Peace is part of the package. It's not dependent on our circumstances or our feelings; it's dependent on our position. I am a daughter of the Prince of Peace. Every child of God has His peace because we have His Spirit.

Now that was something I could stand on. Red-eyed
from the short night, facing students whose loss had just
resurfaced, I had Peace. After bombing an interview, being
stood up by a friend, losing your wallet, or being puked on
by your toddler, you have Peace. In the midst of that dev-
astating diagnosis, totaling your car, closing the casket of a
loved one, or a failed business attempt, you have Peace.

So much of this wilderness journey is a time of redefining. I have discovered the definition for peace: Jesus.

Reflection Questions

What does it mean to you that the *"peace of God transcends all understanding"* (Philippians 4:6-7)?

Recall a time that God has given you indescribable peace
in the middle of chaos or fear.

I suggested that much of the wilderness journey is a time
of redefining. What definitions is God changing for you?

This is Not from the Bible!

IT TOOK ME TWENTY STEPS, fewer if I was running to escape the sleet or hail, to get from our doorstep to the school on the wooden boardwalk. Just off to the left sat the relatively unused, yet revered, Russian Orthodox church. For our first two years, that church only held services on special occasions when a priest would fly in from another village.

We had attended a few out of curiosity and respect for the invitation we'd been given, and we always came away feeling like the symbolism was so rich but completely lost on the attendees. The liturgy was all in Russian; but when, on Easter, we all passed under a tapestry woven with the image of the crucified Christ and marched around the church three times, we fully recognized the attempt to convey the meaning of Jesus' three days in the tomb and our spiritual death and resurrection alongside Him. But when we asked people why they did that ritual, they couldn't explain it at all.

During our third year, a priest and his family moved into our village and regular Sunday services began at the church. Many of the villagers seemed excited about this change and welcomed the priest's family heartily. However, it didn't take us long to discover that they certainly weren't going to be agents of change in the village; instead, they fit right in with the alcoholic tendencies of many of the other families.

The priest's wife signed up to coach our small co-ed basketball team, and things seemed to be going well; but the night before the first tournament at another village, we were given a warning that she was at a party. Her son was a key player on the team, and we wanted to believe that she wouldn't let him down. The next morning, however, when they were supposed to fly out, she didn't show up. She couldn't. She was still too drunk.

Troy quickly packed a bag and hopped on the plane with the team.

Sometime later, Troy was teaching the Cultural Awareness standard of exploring the various explanations of the beginning of the world. He gave fair balance to several stories, allowing the students to draw their own conclusions, but unashamedly answering their direct questions about what he believed. One of the creation stories they explored as a class was from the Bible. Troy printed up Genesis chapter 1 from the New International Version for the students to read together in class. In an attempt to be sensitive to their fierce adherence to Russian Orthodoxy, he gave multiple invitations to the priest to teach the Biblical story of creation, or at least sit in on the class in case students had questions. The priest declined.

The morning after the students read Genesis 1 in class, the priest's wife showed up at school in a complete rage.

She interrupted Troy's class, swearing and shaking the printout of the Biblical creation account.

"What are you trying to teach these kids?" she demanded.

Troy got her to step outside of his classroom and attempted to explain the standard he was teaching. When he told her that the paper she held was from the Bible, she vehemently shot him down.

"This is NOT from the Bible!"

Troy told her that maybe it was a different translation from what she was used to and asked if she could explain how it was different. She had no answer, she just kept berating him for trying to teach the kids a corrupt religion in school.

When Troy assured her that he wasn't trying to cause a problem, he had in fact invited her husband to be part of the discussion, she refused to believe it. The priest was eventually called; and when he showed up, he meekly conceded that Troy had indeed invited him.

His wife was shocked, and her argument deflated. The priest apologized, and Troy returned to his amused class and the priest's embarrassed son. They had an interesting discussion about what is legal in public schools, and how the Bible was originally written in a different language so the various translations can sometimes sound distinct. Probably the most important lesson the kids received that day was the unspoken one of Troy's peace and humility while he was under attack.

The unfortunate lesson that we learned was how the box of Russian Orthodoxy held its followers captive without true understanding, and how we would forever be seen as the enemy if we shared our faith with the kids. And that hurt. After nearly three years of building trust, we didn't feel that the doors were any less locked than they had been in the beginning.

In fact, it seemed we were making things worse.

A couple of months after this, we were invited to a large meal at the house of a woman who had lost her husband several years prior. This meal was to commemorate the anniversary of his passing. This was the typical outlet for both celebration and grief. Celebrating a birthday? Have everyone over for a feast. Mourning a loved one's death? Feed the village. Welcoming a new baby? Gather and eat. Forty days, six months, one year, three years after losing someone? Grieve together over a meal.

Part Russian Orthodox, part Alaskan Native culture, these gatherings were important, so when we were invited, we went. We didn't understand it, we often ate foods we'd rather not, and knowing when to gracefully leave was always awkward, but we still went. They allowed us into their homes and gave us a glimpse into their hearts. These were the times we felt the closest to being accepted into village life.

When we stepped into Kyla's home that day, we were greeted with uncomfortably long hugs. Glazed eyes and loud speech betrayed her inebriation. The brake lines had been cut as this woman's grief mixed with alcohol and her emotions ran full throttle. Only a few other people puttered around her home, some of them giving us apologetic smiles.

We sat at her table, politely filling our plates with samples of the typical spread: fish pie, smoked salmon, sweet rolls, macaroni and cheese, and Jell-O. Whether my memory is clouded with the heaviness of the atmosphere or whether it was actually hazy inside, I can't tell, but it felt dim, dusty, and smothering. Trinkets lined the windowsill behind Troy, an eclectic mix of glass floats, framed photos, figurines, and a child's handmade pottery. Kyla sat across from him, and I sat to the side. She chattered about her late husband, tears welling in her eyes often.

At one point the conversation lulled, and she almost insisted that I help myself to more Tang from the counter behind her. As I got up, she leaned in on her elbows and made eye contact with Troy. "You can't be teachin' our kids your religion. That ain't your job. You do your job and don't be tryin' to teach 'em your Bible. You hear?"

Troy nodded, remaining calm, and assured her that he would do his job. My stomach churned and I wanted to bolt out the door. Somehow, we stayed just long enough after that to thank her for the food and excuse ourselves.

We'd heard tales of previous pastors being met with loaded shotguns on the runway and commanded to get back in their planes and leave. We'd heard Benny and Kim talk about the persecution they'd faced from their family members after turning to Christ a few years ago. But now we felt it, too—not just the resistance, but the adamant opposition.

Jesus called us blessed in Matthew 5:11:

"Blessed are you when people insult you, persecute you and falsely say all kinds of evil against you because of me. Rejoice and be glad, because great is your reward in heaven, for in the same way they persecuted the prophets who were before you."

My spiritual eyes weren't turned enough toward eternity to be able to rejoice in it, though. Mostly it just added to the desperate feeling of banging our heads against closed doors. This begs the question, should you continue in a ministry when it still seems fruitless after several years? Or maybe you need to ask this question after several *months* if you've invested heavily in something, say, a coffee shop outreach, and you need payout in order to even keep your doors open.

There is no pat answer to this question, but I think there are a few guiding principles.

First, wrestle with the Lord over whether He even promised that you would see your desired outcome. Search the scriptures, listen for His voice, and check your motives. Read some past journal entries or emails to loved ones and rediscover the original calling you once felt so strongly. If you believe He has told you that you would see your coffee shop expand into a sort of community center where moms meet to fellowship, teens come to study, and pastors across denominations gather to pray for your city, then hold on to your faith and press on. But do keep asking the Lord to redirect your dream and your methods in any way He sees fit. Have you mingled the call with your own ambitions? Let God strip it back to His vision.

Second, look around for the spiritual impact you *have* had. Chances are, it is greater than you realize, and it might look different than you had envisioned. We thought we were moving to the Alaskan bush to reach hurting kids with the gospel, but I would dare to say that God brought us to that village primarily to encourage Benny and Kim (and to refine our faith—a little purification by fire along the way). How can we possibly measure the worth of one soul?

Luke 15 records three parables that Jesus uses to demonstrate God's extravagant love: a shepherd leaves the ninety-nine sheep to find the one that is lost; a woman sweeps her whole house to find one lost coin; a father welcomes his prodigal son back home. All three stories end with a celebration, a lavish display of love that rejoices over the one. If one soul is worth it in God's book, then one soul sure better be worth it in my book, too.

Third, check your spiritual gauge. If you are not serving out of a place of health, then you probably should step back, at least for a time, to regain your footing on the Solid Rock. Some simple questions, asked frequently of yourself over a period of time, can probably help you assess your spiritual wellness. Is it difficult for me to give thanks? Am I blaming God for my struggles? Do I enjoy spending time with the Lord and do it out of desire, not obligation? If someone asked me what the Lord has been showing me lately, would I have an answer for them? Am I able to rest and receive refreshment from sensing the Lord's nearness and love? Notice, these are questions that primarily test your connection to the Lord. These are different from asking what you learned from the Bible or what you did to serve Jesus today.

It was this last category, the spiritual check, that made us question if we could, or even should, hold to our original five-year plan in this village.

Reflection Questions

Have you ever felt like your best efforts were making things worse?

Wrestle and pray through these questions as you consider your own current service role:

1. What did God originally ask you to do, and are your expectations still in line with His?
2. What spiritual impact *have* you had?
3. Are you able to stay closely connected to the Lord or are you feeling distant from His heart?

Won't You be My Neighbor?

THE TIME TO RENEW OUR contracts for a fourth year of teaching was rapidly approaching, and we had conversation after conversation about what we were going to do. That spiritual gauge was bouncing on the red line.

Troy is highly committal and was willing to stay, but I was tired. Tired of teaching multiple grades, tired of the isolated village life, tired of feeling emotionally battered... just tired. And we wanted to start a family. I knew that if I could barely survive this place by myself, there was no way I could handle it with a baby on my hip. I needed support, and I was no longer ashamed to admit it.

At this point, it was easy to find all the excuses to leave: Troy's mom's heart problems, the inconvenience and frightful prospect of being pregnant in the middle of nowhere, a good chunk of our college loans were paid off, and on and on.

We didn't know what was next, but we decided we would call it quits and return to our hometown after we finished this year.

Then our friends visited. They were the other young couple with our missions' group that had been teaching for two years in the village just a short plane ride north of us. We laughed so much and shared so deeply with them the weekend they stayed with us. Rachel was pregnant, due before the next school year started; and in order to continue teaching the preschool there, she needed someone trust-worthy to watch her baby. Matthew taught the elementary class, and he had heard that the secondary teacher wouldn't be offered his contract for the next year. They did occasional Bible clubs with the kids in the village, and the parents were completely supportive. They had teenagers interested in going to summer Bible camp and asking all kinds of questions about God. In short, the fields were ripe for the harvest, and they just needed more workers.

In what we would come to learn was very typical Matthew fashion, he nonchalantly suggested that maybe the Lord wanted us to live and work alongside them.

And God changed my heart.

It took some talking and praying for my head to consent, but deep within me, my spirit was already whispering *yes* to God's Spirit. That, in and of itself, is an undeniable miracle. Proof, to myself, that God lives within me and has the power to sway my desires.

So, we made a plan. I would gladly step back from teaching and watch Rachel's baby in the mornings while helping Troy with paperwork and other odd jobs in the afternoons. Troy would again be the Head Teacher and teach the 7th through 12th graders. We would live, work, and minister right alongside our dear friends. The school district agreed to our plans, and we moved forward with a new hope that God wasn't finished with us in Alaska just yet.

At this point, I want to pause and revisit the questions I left you—and myself—with early in this book: What happens if I step forward in faith and fall on my face? Can God pick me back up? Can he turn my failure into something good for His name's sake?

Our first yes to God's calling felt mostly like a failed attempt. It wasn't what we expected it would be in terms of our impact in the village or our own ability to handle the challenges of rural Alaska. Saying yes to Him again felt both frightening and promising. I knew from experience that stepping out in faith to serve the Lord could be hard. Like, *really* hard. So, moving to a new village and starting all over again might prove to be more of the same, just in a different setting. But this yes also felt like a second chance. In fact, it felt like it might have been God's plan all along. Had everything we had learned in this first village prepared us to do life much better in the second village?

I had fallen on my face, yes. But God was picking me back up. I had failed in numerous ways, but He was offering the opportunity to redeem those failures and show me how He had strengthened me through them. And in the end, the story is not about my greatness or my success, it is about His glory. If His wisdom and strength is shown through my inability and weakness, then so be it. To God be the glory.

The Author and Perfecter of my faith is a God of restarts, second chances, new beginnings. He invented them, and even before that most poignant display of forgiveness

127

and a fresh start offered on the cross of Christ, the prophet Jeremiah declared, "Because of the Lord's great love we are not consumed, for his compassions never fail. They are new every morning; great is your faithfulness." (Lamentations 3:22-23)

Like the manna on the sand, His compassions are new every morning. Even in this wilderness place—*especially* in this wilderness place—God was demonstrating His sweet mercy to me. We would answer the call a second time. We would step out in faith again. We would trust in His unfailing love, compassion, and faithfulness. Even if we failed by our own measure, He would never fail us. Of this much, I was sure.

Reflection Questions

Have you been afraid to admit that you need support in a particular area? Would it feel like a failure if you asked for help?

How have you experienced God picking you back up when you've messed up?

Do you believe God can use your failures for good? Why or why not?

Great is Thy Faithfulness

THE IDEA OF MOVING TO another village was settling in. We returned from teacher in-service that March feeling like we could wrap up the last two months of teaching well. I still wasn't sure how God had changed my heart so much through His peace; but He had, and I was even kind of excited about it.

About a week after Spring Break, our itinerant Special Education teacher flew in ahead of a snowstorm for her scheduled visit. She was a smiling, five-foot-nothing bundle of determination who was faithfully training for a marathon. We knew the weather didn't look good, so we encouraged her to just run in the gym. She, however, couldn't be deterred by a bit of a blizzard.

Later that night, Troy and I were watching a movie when we got a frantic knock at the door. I don't even remember who it was; but the next thing I knew, Troy was bundling up and heading out in search of our SpEd teacher. The report the messenger carried was terrifying, and I didn't want to believe it was possible. Her gloves had been found on the road about a mile out of the village; and when the young man who discovered them ventured further, he found a body dragged into the bushes. Wolf tracks and blood marred the snow.

The kid hurried back to the village on his snowmobile, and others had gone back to the site where they were circling the body, trying to keep the wolves away. They were too scared by their superstitions to touch her, and the State Troopers wouldn't be there until the morning, if weather permitted. I had no idea what Troy was expected to do in all of this, but I knew he would do whatever needed to be done. And I was scared for him. Scared for everyone out there. Scared to face the reality of what had likely happened to our friend. And yet, what if she was still alive? Had anyone checked her pulse? What kind of terror must she have faced as those animals, each weighing more than she did, closed in on her? Why were her gloves on the road? Had she held up her hands to try to fend them off? Oh, how incredibly frightening. No one nearby to hear her cries for help.

My thoughts whirred, and I felt as if I was in a nightmare. I needed a distraction, so I began washing the dishes. And I prayed scattered, fearful prayers. Finally, as the water and the soap and the grimy dishes mixed and my hands scrubbed and rinsed and scrubbed again, a song found its way to my lips.

Great is Thy Faithfulness, O God my Father.
There is no shadow of turning with Thee.
Thou changest not, Thy compassions they fail not.
As thou hast been thou forever wilt be.[1]

So, I sang and I scoured and I reminded my soul of my Father's unchanging, compassionate nature. Even in this, yes, the most horrific of situations, He is trustworthy.

Troy returned, a long hour later, confirming that it was her. She was dead. Definitely wolves. They'd finally found some men to help move her body until the Troopers could arrive. He needed to call our superintendent.

I kept coming back to that song, anchoring my soul on the only hope possible in this chaos. I was scared to close my eyes because of my vivid imagining of what she must have gone through in her last moments of life, but eventually sleep came.

And so did the morning, dawning with the realization that last night's events were not a nightmare. The storm subsided, the Troopers arrived, and Troy was called in to identify her body, having been given specific information from her family about a tattoo. *Her family.* Oh, how shocked and confused and heartbroken they must be.

Yes, it was her. Was there ever any doubt?

They loaded her body onto the plane, but something faltered in take-off and the plane skidded to a stop on the runway. The villagers said her spirit wasn't ready to leave yet. Fears were running high everywhere.

Then came the hunters. Fish and Game confirmed the wolf attack, and they wanted to eliminate the pack in case of some kind of disease driving them to uncharacteristically kill a human. The villagers tried and failed, so the pros flew in. They found the pack's typical circuit around the lake and basically set an ambush. They then draped the dead wolves over the wing supports of their ski-plane and delivered them to the beach... right outside our window. At the end of two days, eight massive, furry bodies lined the sand. Most of them stretched between six and eight feet long.

I shuddered and closed the blinds until they were gone.

The reports eventually came back, positively identifying two of the largest, healthiest wolves as the killers. We could no longer blame it on disease or starvation in the pack. It was just a freaky fluke. I wanted an excuse, to be able to blame something. Otherwise it just seemed a bit too providential. *Come on, God. That's just horrible. If it was her time to go, couldn't you have used a stroke or something less gruesome?*

After that there were visitors. A couple of reporters. Counselors for the students. A member-care person from our missions' group for us. School-district personnel to address the community at a memorial potluck.

I'm pretty sure I told the pastor that visited us that I was fine. I don't think I was lying; I think I just didn't realize how deeply I was affected by the fear. But my dreams were haunted for weeks; and as I write this, eight years later, I still can't watch a movie with wolf-like creatures in it without being shaken and having subsequent nightmares.

In some ways it seems sadly fitting that this story is essentially the capstone of our time in that village. Whenever people asked about our time there, I could quickly spout off, "Oh it was beautiful, but such a difficult place to live. I mean, there was a murder, arson, and one of our teachers even got killed by wolves!" That pretty much diffused any doubt in people's minds that we were leaving out of our own weakness. I used it as a cover for my feelings of failure.

But I have to caution myself in that tendency. I have to let Jesus rewrite this story on my heart the way He saw it. That is, essentially, what this entire book is about: my attempt to sit with the Lord in these memories and let Him tell me the truth about them. I no longer believe that we failed at our first teaching assignment; rather, I hear Him say that He was using it to refine us and make us more reflective of His glory, not our own.

I've discovered that this practice is incredibly redeeming and healing. Try it sometime. Sit on a park bench or at your kitchen table and grab your journal. If you're like me, a coffee shop and your laptop will do. But you need to write it down, even if writing isn't a strength of yours; seeing it concretely before you and being able to reread it is key. Begin by telling the Lord that you are inviting Him to retell you your story as you write, and just start remembering. Don't censor it. Recall all the feelings and the questions from whatever painful memory you need to bring into the light.

Give yourself plenty of time, and listen to those promptings where the Spirit says, "Wait. That's not how I see it."

Ask Him for scriptural truth to replace the lies you've told yourself over and over again in relation to that memory and ask Him to show you what He was planting in your own heart that might now be starting to grow. Ask Him to show you how He was demonstrating His love or His mercy. There is no story of your life that does not bear His fingerprints. So don't be afraid. Ask Him to reveal His faithfulness, and He will. He will.

Great is Thy faithfulness,
Great is Thy faithfulness,
Morning by morning new mercies I see.
All I have needed Thy hand hath provided.
Great is Thy faithfulness
Lord unto me.

Reflection Questions

Do you find it difficult to declare that God is faithful and trustworthy amid horrific situations?

Have you ever asked Jesus to retell you a difficult experience through His eyes? Why don't you try it right now?

Whose woods these are I think I know.

His house is in the village though;

He will not see me stopping here

To watch his woods fill up with snow.

My little horse must think it queer

To stop without a farmhouse near

Between the woods and frozen lake

The darkest evening of the year.

He gives his harness bells a shake

To ask if there is some mistake.

The only other sound's the sweep

Of easy wind and downy flake.

The woods are lovely, dark and deep,

But I have promises to keep,

COLLIDING WITH THE CALL

And miles to go before I sleep,
And miles to go before I sleep.

— Robert Frost,
"STOPPING BY WOODS ON A SNOWY EVENING"[1]

Sand Me Smooth

WE WERE ONLY 101 MILES away from our first teaching assignment, but we landed in a whole new world when we returned to the bush for our fourth year. This second village was as flat as our first one was mountainous; as open to the gospel as our first one was resistant; and as laughter filled as our first one was tear filled.

Several years back, after a particularly traumatic series of events here, one of the influential elders told the village that what they were doing wasn't working. They needed to welcome in more Christian influence, because she had seen that make a difference in other places where her family lived. Ironically, this elder was the sister to one of the ladies from our first village. Clearly, that wasn't the place of improvement she was referring to. There had been a lot of openness and growth over the recent past here; and although the village was small, it had some good people who worked hard to keep things from getting out of control again.

We had a clinic staffed by a trained Health Aide, who also happened to be a believer. We had a Village Personal Safety Officer, whose family loosely maintained their Christian background. We had a generous couple, that held a lot of sway in the village, that expressly supported the school and frequently invited the teachers to their home. And, most importantly, we had teammates. We would live, work, and minister right alongside Matthew and Rachel, who had already been here for two years.

Before we arrived in the village, we were at a regional mission's conference where we received some advice from two other women who had been partnering in a small village for several years already. They gently instructed us to go into this relationship as we would a marriage: committed, recognizing that neither of us is perfect, and prepared to be quick to forgive. We grabbed on to that wisdom, discussed some boundaries and safeguards, and dove into our ministry marriage.

It turned out to be the most close-knit, unique relationship we have ever experienced with another couple. We shared the same frustrations and joys in our village-life bubble; and we made the most of the limited space we had by going for walks outside when the weather was nice, or pacing the gym on the frequent days when the rain came down sideways. We shared many meals together, watched silly movies together, planned school activities together, and played pickleball on the basketball court together. That was our life. *Together* epitomized pretty much everything; and after three years of *lonely* being our trademark, we eagerly gobbled up this life-giving partnership.

Had we started out with teammates when we arrived in Alaska, we might not have struggled so much through those first three years. However, I believe that the comradery was sweeter and healthier because of those difficult initial years.

When we stepped into our new roles in this village, I completely shed my skin as a teacher and began the process of molting into something different, something harder to define.

I was more than ready to let go of the stress and exhaustion of being a full-time elementary teacher, but I wasn't ready to let go of the label. The comfort of having a quick definition for who you are and what you do is easy to cling to. And after the tens of thousands of dollars we spent to get my degree and my teacher tag, I couldn't just lay it aside, could I?

Yet I knew I was called to something new, and I found it strangely satisfying to be able to help and support my husband, teammates, and the students in a variety of ways. Troy was the Head Teacher again, but I was his unpaid secretary. I spent hours organizing the files in the office and continued to keep track of the monthly paperwork requirements for that first year. I had a paid position as a classroom aide in Troy's room for one hour each morning, after which time I would pick up Rachel's four-month-old son and take care of him in our home for three hours while she taught preschool. There were a couple of times I subbed in Matthew's classroom, and numerous times that I became the "bus" driver.

The school bus was a tired Suburban that made its rounds through the two-mile spread of village each morning and afternoon. For the first couple of months, the morning rounds were in the daylight, then for a while they were right at sunrise. This was my favorite time of year to be out picking the kids up, because those sunrises behind the distant volcano were breathtaking, always lifting my spirits heavenward. As the winter months neared, the morning drive became pre-dawn, and I would often catch foxes dashing across the road in the headlights. I enjoyed being the first one to greet the kids in the morning. Some of them would chat with me, some of them would sit there in a sleepy heap, but they were all welcomed into that Suburban by name. It felt good to love them in this simple way.

Perhaps in previous years I would have felt insignificant in my roles as aide, babysitter, bus driver, and substitute; but God gave me the grace to embrace the opportunity of that season to be in a support role. If you've ever done something really hard and felt utterly alone in it, you know how incredible it feels when someone comes along and figuratively holds your arms up so you can continue your work. Moses felt this way, too.

"So Joshua did what Moses had commanded and fought the army of Amalek. Meanwhile, Moses, Aaron, and Hur climbed to the top of a nearby hill. As long as Moses held up the staff in his hand, the Israelites had the advantage. But whenever he dropped his hand, the Amalekites gained the advantage. Moses' arms soon became so tired he could no longer hold them up. So Aaron and Hur found a stone for him to sit on. Then they stood on each side of Moses, holding up his hands. So his hands held steady until sunset. As a result, Joshua overwhelmed the army of Amalek in battle."

EXODUS 17:10-13

I got to be Aaron in this season. Or maybe Hur, but I like the name Aaron better, so we'll go with that. And as Joshua is a pre-figure of Christ, I can testify that Jesus was the one doing the battling in our village. We all just stood there and tried to help one another obey what the Lord asked us to do. We raised the banner of Yahweh, and ground was won for His kingdom.

The keen reminder of the past three years of struggling alone, unable to keep my arms from dragging on the ground, made it that much easier to embrace the idea of standing together in unity so that we could be part of what God was working to accomplish around us. I was not insignificant in my support role, of that much I was sure.

For years, I would still identify myself as a teacher. Occasionally I still do, but that year was the beginning of discovering the beauty of serving. Coming alongside others in unified partnership became a new passion of ours. I was becoming a servant—the kind that Phil called out in us back at that fish wheel on our vision trip. A servant who loves for love's sake, not for her own self-fulfillment.

Something had been broken in me during our struggles in the first village. A portion of my pride and my stubborn independence had been crushed. The grief, the frustration,

145

and the persecution were painful, but the Master used them to teach me to rely more deeply on Him.

Sadly, I still like to think of myself as self-sufficient, self-directed, self-starting, self-correcting, self-assured... self, self, self. The world tells me these are good things. My own experience with others tells me these are good things. Most of the people I look up to teach themselves a great deal; they don't need others to remind them to finish a task; they are what I would call reliable, dependable, go-getters. I like to identify myself with them. It's part of how I'm wired, I believe, with God-given gifts of responsibility and creativity that are good. Until they're not. Until I forget Who gave them to me and depend on my own strength, not His.

I don't believe that God in any way wants to diminish or squash these abilities; rather, He wants to polish them until they shine and reflect His goodness and love. And that's where the rub of those sandpaper experiences comes in.

My dad is a carpenter—the kind of carpenter that starts with a tree and ends with a home. He doesn't frequent the building supply stores so much as he frequents the woods with a saw. He has designed and built 23 houses, and over a dozen garages, barns, and various outbuildings.

One of the greatest privileges of my life has been working alongside him to build a home of our own. When we framed it up, any old rough two by four would do. But when we did the finishing work on the cabinets, we spent days sanding. Sawdust would coat our hair and eyelashes and be swept up into great piles after those long hours of sanding. First the rough grit, then the medium grit, and finally the fine grit would make the wood ever smoother until it felt almost like silk. These are the surfaces that we touch, that others touch, that you don't want to constantly get splinters from. These are the pieces we live our lives out of and the places where our handiwork can be most clearly seen. The measure of our care is on display in those cabinets.

And so it is with God. We are the display of His glory, and He loves us, and those we come in contact with, too much to leave us all rough and splintery. In His skilled hands, the trials smooth away the sinful knots, the course pride, and the piercing insecurities. The abrasion hurts, and we don't have to like it; but we can look ahead to the end product and trust the Carpenter to do what is for our good, that His beauty might be reflected in us.

While our first village was about as rough a grit as sandpaper gets, He used it to wear down that top layer of *self* that was so prominent on my features. And He's not done. That's both comforting and scary to say. More sanding means more discomfort, but it also means that He cares, and He'll patiently work down my self-reliance until my features show God-reliance. He'll take my abilities—those things he gave me to begin with—and make sure I don't injure myself or others with a splintering version.

147

Just like my dad does, just like Jesus did while assisting Joseph in his carpentry work, Father God is taking a tree and making a home. A home for His Spirit. A home for His glory.

Reflection Questions

Are there any titles or labels that you've earned that you're finding hard to let go of when God leads you in a different direction?

What "self" words do you use to define yourself? Do any of these indicate areas of pride or idolatry in your heart?

What sandpaper trials can you give thanks for, recognizing how God has used them to polish you until you shine for His glory?

The Womb

WE WERE NOW PART OF a village team, a regional team, an organizational team, and a unique subgroup of teacher-missionaries. Times we could gather with these larger groups were sparse, but special.

It seemed that we always grumbled, at least inwardly, at making time for the big regional gatherings and trainings, but some of my favorite memories came from those times. Like when they brought in an incredibly talented speaker and pianist who could create impromptu songs and make us all laugh with their hilarity and cleverness. Or when another speaker shared a moving story and a question that the Spirit used to push me through the next year: *Is Jesus worthy of even this?*

Before we left the shores of familiarity for another school year of riding the waves of isolation in uncharted waters, we could picnic on the beach of camaraderie for just a little while. For two years there were four teacher-missionary units in our organization. And one of those years, we were all either pregnant or hoping to be soon. So "The Great Baby Race" began. Jokes abounded, fears of going into labor too soon in the village were shared, hopes for our children's futures were acknowledged, and we forged yet another strong connecting point with our team of teachers. In one more way, we were all in this together, no matter how geographically spread out we were.

149

Our regional team was a bit more diverse in age, vocation, and length of time in Alaska; but when we would get together over school in-services or holidays, it felt like coming home. We were a family. And we loved staying in the homes of our teammates who lived in the bigger village, especially in one windowless, basement guest room that we affectionately named "The Womb." It was dark, it was cozy, and it was filled with love. We knew we were always welcome there.

I can still smell the baked oatmeal in the kitchen upstairs, see the spruce trees out the bay window from my perch atop their elliptical machine, feel the soft fur and the wet tongue of their husky, and hear my voice lilting as I read a children's book to their son, curled up under a crocheted blanket on the couch. Around their table we played games and laughed until we cried, and we shared those deep places of heartache that we knew very few others could understand.

A life that thrives is one that is born out of a family.

A healthy family accepts each member as they are, while supporting them to grow.

A family sees the potential carried in each other and speaks it into existence through words of encouragement and exhortation.

A family feels each other's pain and doesn't leave anyone to cry alone.

A family is a safe place to bring your mess and ask for help.

Each member of the family has a different role, and the ones farther along in the growth process hold the hand of the younger ones without shaming them for their lack of ability to walk upright on their own yet. But they also celebrate every independent step toward maturity.

In our team-family, our hearts found a home to grow in, and we discovered how beautiful it is to need each other. We had a place to be heard and to heal. A place to belong.

I know not every team functions as a healthy family. Our generation is wrought with more broken families—in both the natural and the spiritual—than probably ever before. Saying you come from a dysfunctional family is laughable. Don't we all? And the enemy of our souls gloats over his success in this area. Without healthy family, it is very difficult to develop well. Satan has stunted our growth, as individuals and as local churches and missions, by destroying our concept of and trust in family.

As I write this, we are in the process of adopting a child from Thailand. Here, it's a very long, uncertain road. It's been two and a half years since we turned in our application, and we haven't heard anything from our social worker since our home study a year and a half ago. We already have two incredible and exhausting children and plenty of challenges living overseas. So why on earth would we subject ourselves to the paperwork, the waiting, and the rearranging of our lives that adoption causes? I have to re-ask and re-answer this question to myself over and over again.

But the answer really is quite simple: family. God created us for family, and just as He has adopted me into His own family, causing all kinds of upheaval and pain on His own part, I want to give family to a child who has none. No matter the cost. For me, it's a matter of obedience. And, as you now know, my past choices to obey have led me to some pretty hard places. I expect nothing different from this.

Orphans get all kinds of lovely labels to explain their irregular growth, such as "failure to thrive" and "institutional delays". Basically, as near as I can tell, all those mean is that they weren't raised in a loving family. A safe place to explore, a nurturing environment to learn, and a protective embrace to call their own have all been denied. Family. It's everything.

In our teams and organizations, we need to be looking for ways to create that sense of security and belonging that comes from family. I don't know that we need more clearly crafted vision statements and five-year growth plans so much as we need brothers to teach us how to build tall towers like them and mothers to hold us when we're sad that our tower fell down. We need sisters to share secrets and

152

dreams with and fathers to warn the sketchy prom date with a severe look when we haven't chosen so wisely.

If you don't have this in your team, can you be the one to initiate it, asking someone to mentor you, inviting co-workers over for dinner, or just showing up at the important events in another person's life? Can you be that mother or father or sister or brother that someone needs? Or can you humble yourself enough to tell your leaders that you're struggling and you'd like their help?

We're not designed to be Lone Rangers; we're destined to be The Avengers—a formidable team of heroes battling side by side, each using our own specific abilities to help the rest. The evil we face will decimate us if we tackle it alone. We need the whole cloud of witnesses and our fearless leader, Jesus, to overcome.[1] So find your family or create your family, and step into a place of safety and healing unlike any other.

Think of the healthiest family, team, or community you have ever been a part of. What are its defining characteristics?

Have you ever considered adoption—physically or spiritually inviting someone into your family? Why or why not?

How have you found healing in community?

This is My Body

IN SPITE OF THE GREATER ease we had in living here, village life was far from perfect. Just across the road from the school stood one of the more infamous party houses. An older white guy lived there; and even though it felt like nobody really trusted him, he was accepted and perhaps even revered to a degree for the influence he held as a supplier of alcohol, and most likely drugs, as well.

Sometimes, we would meet the airplane at the runway to pick up an itinerant worker or a large box we were expecting, and we would see case after case of alcohol being delivered. We would know that a big party was in the works, and we would pray that nothing would get out of hand.

One night, thanks to my pregnancy, I was up late to use the bathroom. I heard hollering coming from outside, and I cracked the window to listen to what was going on. A door slammed, and a female voice cried out in complete despair, "I hate myself!" My heart broke. I woke Troy and we hurried outside to see if this girl needed help, but she was nowhere to be seen. The lights were still on in the house across the road. We could only imagine what had happened, but we were helpless to do anything.

The next day we asked a few people we trusted about what was going on the night before. We confirmed there had been a party, but no one knew of anything out of the

155

ordinary happening. Relief washed over us as we thanked God that this woman hadn't acted out in her despair and self-hatred. Alaska holds the record for suicide, so we had reason to fear, but thankfully nothing was attempted that night.

We had ten to twelve students in the entire school from about four main families in our village. It was impossible not to learn about their history. We knew about divorce, about sibling death, about physical abuse and molestation and incest, about estranged family members, and about all the wounds that come with having alcoholic parents. We heard about the nights our students couldn't sleep because their parents were fighting, the disgustingly violent video games their younger siblings were allowed to play, and their very real fears of losing a loved one again. We felt like we knew so much, and yet really, we were just new-comers—outsiders who only saw the tip of the iceberg.

The year before we moved to this village, one boy in his early teens, decided to follow Jesus at a summer Bible camp. Wade wasn't exactly an amazing student, nor did he have a very good home life. His emotional baggage was big, but his heart for Jesus was bigger. And we just knew that, if for no other reason, God wanted us there to encourage him. For four years Troy taught him in the classroom, coached him on the sports court, and discipled him in matters of everyday life. They could be ridiculously goofy together and they could cry together. They sometimes drove each other nuts.

God gave them a bond that lasts to this day. Wade still contacts us when he's really struggling and needs prayer, and we are so very thankful for his growing love for Jesus. God is going to use this young man to reach his family and his people yet.

He is one story of hope among many others of sorrow. But whether the pain felt heavy, or the generational abuse felt hopeless, or the fear of impending trauma felt frightening, we knew one thing. This was part of loving our students: shouldering these feelings and fears with them.

There are some pretty clear biblical mandates on loving others well. Galatians 6:2 says, "Carry each other's burdens, and in this way you will fulfill the law of Christ." Romans 12:15 says, "Rejoice with those who rejoice; mourn with those who mourn." Both are written by Paul, and both verses are immediately followed with a call to humility: "If anyone thinks they are something when they are not, they deceive themselves," (Galatians 6:3) and, "Live in harmony with one another. Do not be proud, but be willing to associate with people of low position. Do not be conceited." (Romans 12:16)

My own paraphrase of these four verses might sound something like this: Don't for a minute think that you are too good or too important to slow down and sit with someone else in the middle of their pain or to do a happy dance with them in their joy. That's where Christ's real love is found.

I bristle against it. The call to get my hands dirty in the mess of someone else's life.

My Western, individualistic mindset clashes with the Word and the heart of God. Because if I look back just a little bit earlier in the Romans section, I find something truly revealing about *why* I am to share in the life of another. Verse five floors me with, "So in Christ we, though many, form one body. And each member belongs to all the others." At least eight other times in his letters, Paul mentioned the idea of all believers forming one body.

So, the way God sees it, their pain *is* my pain. Their joy *is* my joy. And the inverse is true, too. My sufferings, my victories, and all my mundane steps in between belong to the body. If I stub my toe, I might say "My toe hurts," or I might say, "I'm hurt." Both are equally true. So, when I think I can somehow shield myself from another person's pain by simply ignoring it, I'm deluding myself. It's already my pain if they are in Christ, and somehow my acknowledging that and shouldering it with them softens the blow.

Carrying one another's burdens is daunting, though. It's almost always more than I can handle. This is where I must remember that I'm not taking this on alone—it's a whole-body effort. More than that, Jesus wants to carry these burdens with us, even for us. We can't forget the comfort of 1 Peter 5:7, which reminds us to "cast all your anxiety on him for he cares for you."

It's a great mystery how Christ invites us to partake of His body, to share in His sufferings. Let's take a minute to examine one of the most divisive, outlandish teachings that Jesus made while on this earth. Shortly after feeding 5,000 men, plus women and children, and walking on water, Jesus said:

"I am the bread of life. Your ancestors ate the manna in the wilderness, yet they died. But here is the bread that comes down from heaven, which anyone may eat and not die. I am the living bread that came down from heaven. Whoever eats this bread will live forever. This bread is my flesh, which I will give for the life of the world."

Then the Jews began to argue sharply among themselves, "How can this man give us his flesh to eat?"

Jesus said to them, "Very truly I tell you, unless you eat the flesh of the Son of Man and drink his blood, you have no life in you. Whoever eats my flesh and drinks my blood has eternal life, and I will raise them up at the last day. For my flesh is real food and my blood is real drink. Whoever eats my flesh and drinks my blood remains in me, and I in them. Just as the living Father sent me and I live because of the Father, so the one who feeds on me will live because of me. This is the bread that came down from heaven. Your ancestors ate manna and died, but whoever feeds on this bread will live forever."

JOHN 6:48-58

Yes, Jesus sounds pretty insane here. It brings to mind C.S. Lewis's famous apologetic argument[1], challenging us to recognize that Jesus is either Lord (truly who He says He is), a liar (deceiving people for his own gain), or a complete lunatic (who actually believed the words he said). There's really no middle ground allowing Him to simply be a prophet or a good teacher. His self-claims were too extreme for that.

So, what does Jesus mean when he tells us that if we eat his flesh and drink his blood, we will have eternal life? Is it just an acknowledgment that He is the only One to save us from sin and death? Is it an invitation to live an upright life, following God's moral code like He did? Is it simply a foreshadowing of the last supper and our human need to regularly remember His sacrifice, lest we forget?

I tend to think it has more to do with the remaining, the abiding, the daily consuming, the insatiable desire for Jesus. It's an invitation to be all in. My life is dependent on His life. His life is my life. We are inseparable—one body.

Later, John records some of Jesus' final prayers. "My prayer is not for them alone. I pray also for those who will believe in me through their message, that all of them may be one, Father, just as you are in me and I am in you. May they also be in us so that the world may believe that you have sent me. I have given them the glory that you gave me, that they may be one as we are one—I in them and you in me—so that they may be brought to complete unity. Then the world will know that you sent me and have loved them even as you have loved me." (John 17:20-23)

There it is. Sweetly and perfectly, a prayer for you and me from the lips of our Savior. First and foremost, He desires that we would be united to Him; and in that miraculous entwining of our lives with His, we become one with each other, too. And the resulting testimony of this unity? *That the world may believe.* Oh, that His body would walk in solitary pursuit of knowing God and seeing God's kingdom come and His will be done on earth as it is in heaven! Let it be so, Lord. Let it be so.

Reflection Questions

How do you feel about getting your hands dirty in the mess of someone else's life?

What thoughts and feelings are stirring in you as you consider being part of the global, timeless body of Christ?

What is your prayer for the unity of believers?

Circles

I GLANCED AT THE CLOCK while changing my son's
diaper. He stretched his pudgy fist into the air and fussed.
"I know, Tiger. Hang in there. You get to take your nap
in the stroller today."

Chanan smiled at my playful tone and squirmed at just
the right time to make me lose my grip on the Velcro tab.
*Sheesh. You'd think that after doing this diaper thing ump-
teen times a day for the last four months I'd have it down.*
I refastened the tab and stuffed my son into a fuzzy, full-
body suit complete with ears on the hood. He was now a
living teddy bear.

I nestled him into the three-wheeled, large-tired stroller
and quickly yanked on my snow gear. November in Alaska
is no joke, but after a week of sideways-blown sleet, today's sunshine was too tantalizing to resist. Stroller hood
down, additional weather cover secured, and we were
ready. I peeked out the window and saw Rachel exit her
house with her one-and-a-half-year-old son strapped in his
own armored tank of a stroller.

"Let's go, Buddy. I sure hope you fall asleep quickly,"
I murmured. Getting this colicky kid to sleep had become
the most brutal training ground in patience I had ever experienced. One of the only things that soothed his
temperamental tummy and feisty spirit was bouncing. Up
and down and up and down while I paced the house back

163

and forth and back and forth. "Since you didn't sleep much last night, you can make up for it with a nice long nap, okay?" I sighed. *Wishful thinking.*

I opened the door and was greeted with nose-biting air and gleaming light angled from the sun's sleepy position just over the horizon line, even though it was midday. Pale blue sky, mottled brown and white snowy tundra, and grayed-wood buildings complimented each other's muted tones. Rachel and I pushed our go-anywhere strollers onto the road and chatted while the gravel and ice chunks bounced our boys to sleep. The "loop" took us past the school, up the hill that overlooked the bay, around the corner to the straight stretch near the runway, and to the Post Office, which marked halfway. We knew there wouldn't be any mail since the plane hadn't come yet today, but we stopped at the Post Office anyway to greet Carol and let our cheeks thaw.

Wanting to finish the lap before a hungry baby woke up, we walked a bit faster as we completed the circuit that curved past a cluster of homes and the old airport before arriving right back where we started. One big circle. But it sure beat the dozens of smaller circles we had done in the gym a few days prior. We would likely wear the floor finish into a groove before winter was over in an attempt to maintain our sanity and stave off cabin fever.

Circles, pacing, bouncing, and the endless cycle of diapers and feeding made my life feel like a rerun day after day. Can I get an amen from every new mom in history?

And as we'd now entered our fifth year teaching in the bush, even the school year felt predictable and redundant. This was a season of repetition. And for a girl who styles her hair differently every single day, the monotony did not settle well with me.

We like to map out life on a timeline, but it's rarely linear. Life is marked by ups and downs, twists and turns, two steps forward and three steps back. We think we've learned something only to find out we need to reassess our knowledge from a completely new angle the next time we revisit it. We get stuck in negative cycles and spiral downward in our spiritual or emotional journey. We go in circles.

Maybe what we think of as a two-dimensional circle is really a three-dimensional globe, but like wrapping up a ball of yarn, we can only comprehend one string at a time. God, however, sees things differently. I'm going to steal my husband's favorite analogy for helping his students consider the difference between their perspective and the Creator's. First, he has them draw a stick figure on a piece of paper and call him Joe. "Now," he says, holding up a ball, "draw this ball for Joe in a way he can understand." They draw circles. They try to partially shade them in to show dimension. A few might even try to remember the geometric equation for a sphere and write that down. "How does what you drew on your paper compare to this ball?" he asks. "Does Joe understand what it feels like to hold a ball, or the variety of sizes, colors, and textures a ball can come in?" They shake their heads. "And he never really will, because Joe is only 2D and this ball is 3D." Then they contemplate together the vast difference between their own three-dimensional experience and whatever multi-dimension we might imagine God to operate in. It's a fun exercise, and it bears a strong significance on our lives.

You see, walking in circles is as old as time, and it's not without its purposes as God Almighty slowly and patiently retrains us to see things more from His perspective. With each lap, each loop, and every strand wound around the ball of our lives, we more fully feel the nuances and shape of God's intentions and plans.

So here I am again, circling back to the experience of the Israelites as they wandered in the wilderness.

Only they weren't really wandering, were they? They were being led. "In all the travels of the Israelites, when-ever the cloud lifted from above the tabernacle, they would set out; but if the cloud did not lift, they did not set out—until the day it lifted. So the cloud of the Lord was over the tabernacle by day, and fire was in the cloud by night, in the sight of all the Israelites during all their travels." These are the concluding verses of the entire book of Exodus (40:36-38). God directed them as they did their wilderness laps; and with every set-up and tear-down of their camp, their obedience to the Lord was being reinforced.

Allow me to bring in another circular training compari-son from my youth: the round pen. I grew up with horses and had grand delusions that I was a qualified horse trainer. My crazy but faithful pony served me well as I grew up, but in my pre-teen years my dad bought me a yearling Quarter Horse at an auction. Now, I wasn't expecting an untrained yearling. I wanted a horse I could ride. But the trained horses were a bit out of our price range, so I got a young, long-legged bay with a star on his forehead. My dad and I did some research and learned that there were two things I could do to begin training this playful gelding without riding him. First, I could lead him around. I'd snap the rope to his halter and take him on walks in the woods. We'd practice "whoa" and "walk on." We'd turn left and right. We'd back up. He'd try to rip my eleven-year old arm off to snag a bite of grass. I'd click my tongue furiously and we'd keep going.

The second thing we did was build a round pen. Nothing more than a gated circle, this was where my horse, nicknamed Jay, would learn to depend on me to direct his movement. I read about all the lunging techniques in my stacks of horse magazines and set out to teach Jay to walk, trot, canter, and reverse on my command. And I loved it. I loved watching him start out all full of fire, tossing his mane, kicking out his rear legs, dashing in frantic circles as I steadily coaxed him onward with a mere flick of the lunge whip.

Then he'd slow down, sweat lathered across his chest, and start turning his ears toward me. Once I had his attention we'd work on the cues. He'd go in circles and we'd repeat the drill over and over and over again. By the end of two years, when he was ready for saddle, he knew both my verbal cues and my body language. One click of my tongue with a slight arm gesture and he'd increase speed. A change in my body angle to step ever so slightly in front of his line of vision and he'd slow down. And if I stood still, he'd walk right up to me and wait for me to scratch under his mane and praise him.

Repetition reinforces the message the trainer is trying to instill. Going in circles works.

We are creatures prone to wander, likely to forget. But we are also creatures of habit. If we do something enough times—whether good or bad—it becomes ingrained in us, and soon we are repeating it without even realizing it. And I'm so glad. If I had to reteach my fingers where the letters are on the keyboard every time I sat down to write, this book would never get finished. Instead, my fingers and QWERTY never forget each other. It's called muscle memory. And I believe there is such a thing as spiritual memory, too.

More than mere mental recollection, habits can be deeply ingrained in our spirits. Every time I choose to trust God in a difficult situation, I reinforce in my spirit that He is trustworthy. Soon, I'm no longer reminding myself that He's trustworthy; I'm unwaveringly confident in it. My spirit remembers His faithfulness.

So, what was God reinforcing in my spirit through the redundancy of the laps I paced with our first born during this season in Alaska? Well, unrelenting, sacrificial, tire-less love, for one. A glimpse of His father-heart that never gives up, that holds us when we're unsettled and too tired to sleep, that sees the fleeting days of our current stage and holds on expectantly to the joy of the next new milestone ahead. Just as He was with the Israelites during their wilderness laps, He was with me in mine. And He is with you in yours.

The Lord is a good trainer.

Reflection Questions

Recall a season of your life that felt particularly redundant. Can you identify a lesson God was ingraining deep in your spirit during that time?

How does it move you to know that in the concluding verses of Exodus, we are told that the Israelites were not actually wandering in the wilderness, they were being led?

What lesson keeps resurfacing in your life in your current season? Thank God for patiently training you in godliness.

A Shouting God

I DON'T KNOW WHO FIRST came up with the idea; but early in our 2nd year there, while I still had a nursing baby, the high schoolers decided they wanted to take a school trip to Hawaii. And somehow, they got us to agree to it. We knew it would take a lot of fundraising and a big commitment on our part, but we also knew it would be an eye-opening opportunity for the kids and a relationship building opportunity for us.

At that time, we had a highly motivated pair of sisters that helped push the planning and fundraising along. They wrangled their cousins and friends into baking for bake sales, cooking and serving at "restaurant nights" in the gymnasium, and selling raffle tickets for donated prizes. And, somehow, all that plus gifts from family and friends paid for nine students and four chaperones to go to the Big Island right after school ended for the year in May.

I oversaw purchasing the plane tickets, and, thankfully, there are always special sales from Alaska to Hawaii. Go figure. A couple of months before departure the students brought us their signed permission slips as their commitment to go, and I locked in the tickets. Everyone was excited. Then, the morning that we were leaving, I got a call from Melissa, a girl I had done some Bible study with earlier in the year. She wasn't going to come.

171

Seriously? You were ecstatic yesterday, then today you decide to back out? I couldn't get a full explanation from her, nor could I talk her into changing her mind. Rumors flew: she didn't want to give up smoking while on the trip; she was too scared to fly; she didn't want to spend that much time near her ex-boyfriend. But it didn't really matter what her reason was. No one could convince her to come.

We made a snap decision to invite the kid who had shown up in town just a few weeks ago in her stead, if I could get the ticket changed. Here, I have to give credit to this particular airline. I may have had to talk to five different people over the phone, but eventually, they did allow us to change the name on her ticket so this other boy could come. He was packed and ready in minutes, and we all gathered in the school to await the radio call that our airplane had arrived.

Leg number one took us to the hub village north of us. Leg number two was to Anchorage. And the final leg was to Honolulu. All in all, travel was as smooth as could be expected.

At this time, Chanan was ten months old, Rachel's son was just over two, and she was pregnant with their second. Our children were pretty resilient travelers, but we knew we couldn't keep up with the jam-packed itinerary of sightseeing and adventures; so we scheduled in a couple of days for us to stay behind and prepare a meal for the kids to come home to.

Home was a large, single-story house that we were able to rent for a reasonable price. Kids were draped across couches and crammed into beds, but it really worked out quite nicely as we bumped into each other and bonded family-style. You learn things about people you stay overnight with that you likely never would otherwise, like who talked in their sleep and who hated the smell of mango. We got video footage of the colorful spider in the backyard and of giddy Alaskans splashing in the warm ocean for the first time.

We attempted snorkeling, rocked go-karting, toured Pearl Harbor, and kayaked the bay. It was beyond precious to watch their reactions to trying new tropical fruits and simply taking in the excitement of the city. One of the most expensive and highly anticipated activities planned was a dunk in the shark cage out in the deep waters of the sea. Rachel and I were clearly planning to stay behind with our little kids for this adventure, but as it turned out, nobody got to go.

The night before the shark experience, one of our most responsible students brought us an empty canister of chewing tobacco that she had found under the towels in the shared bathroom. The expectations were loud and clear that absolutely no substances would be tolerated on this trip. We had no way to prove whose it was, so we decided to try to get a confession. Either one person could own up to it and suffer the consequences, or the whole group would be punished with a long run on the beach and the cancellation of our shark encounter. Fingers were pointed, and suspicions were shared; but no one could prove anything, and no one confessed.

That was a sad, sad day. Especially for the girl who brought the can to our attention. She and her sister had been the ones to put the most effort into the fundraising for this trip, and she was perhaps the most excited about seeing the sharks. She didn't have to show us that chewing tobacco. She could have thrown it away and protected her friends and the trip. But she chose integrity, and we were so proud of her. The converse of her honesty was the fear and selfishness shown by whoever chose to let the group suffer rather than owning their consequence. It was hard for us not to hold bitterness in our hearts toward the kid we strongly suspected was responsible.

In the end, it was a painful testament to the destructive grip that substance abuse has on so many Alaskan villages. Even the youth. And if we really want to point a finger, let's point it back in our own faces and recognize that it was our forerunners, the Russians and the American gold-rushers, who brought these substances to the Native Alaskans in the first place. We traded alcohol for fur and tobacco for labor. We may not have put them on reservations up there, but we forever altered their freedom to live off the land by enslaving them to modern conveniences. All too often now, spam replaces frozen meat and fetal alcohol syndrome replaces ingenuity and survival skills.

I'm not a social activist. I don't think all the ways of the Western World are evil. Globalization is a fact, and education is critical in today's age. But after sitting with grandmas who were slapped across the mouth in school if they spoke their mother tongue, and crying with students who lost family to parties gone awry, I've learned to feel their loss and accept my responsibility in it. My culture has dominated theirs, and living with that grief has hurt them in more ways than I will ever understand.

The frustration of losing the shark encounter over someone's addiction and stubbornness caused us to have some significant group discussions about responsibility and forgiveness. For that, I am thankful. I suspect that many of them learned more through that failure than they did through all the other positive experiences of the trip. Isn't that just how life often works? C.S. Lewis sums it up well:

"God whispers to us in our pleasures, speaks in our conscience, but shouts in our pains: it is his megaphone to rouse a deaf world."[1]

In all this, my heart is reminded to cry out for the pain of addiction, loss, and abuse to open the ears of the Alaskan Natives—and the inner city kids, the farming families, the affluent professionals, my own family—to the One who is making all things new. So, I'm changing the way I pray.

If pain is one of our greatest teachers, and if God allows it that we might see His beauty and yearn for His touch, then maybe I shouldn't always ask that the pain be taken away. Maybe I should stop assuming that God's greatest desire is our happiness, our comfort. If His heart is for our holiness, then perhaps we need the pain.

My prayers now go a bit more like this: May we hear you in the pain, Lord Jesus. If you will, take this cup, yet not my will, but yours be done.

Reflection Questions

What do you think of C.S. Lewis' quote: *"God whispers to us in our pleasures, speaks in our conscience, but shouts in our pains: it is his megaphone to rouse a deaf world."*?

How has seeing God's faithfulness and purpose in pain changed the nature of your prayers?

What do you need to pray "not my will, but Yours be done," over today?

Will the Plane Come Today?

LAST NIGHT WE HAD SOME friends over for dinner—
fellow missionary teachers with us in Thailand. One of at
least ten families that we connect well with, that we fellowship regularly with, that we partner for the sake of the
gospel with every day. That's not to mention the dozens of
others that we have a smile-and-wave kind of passing relationship with. We were chatting about making friendships
cross-culturally and the language and social challenges that
come with that, when Troy recalled how different it was
being so isolated in Alaska.

We would go for weeks looking at only each other, our
co-teachers, and the same dozen student faces. Those beautiful faces, round like a blueberry, tinted with the warm hue
of earth. Faces framed in raven hair, set with dark eyes that
changed like the sky, often cloudy and veiled, then the next
moment streaked with angry lightening. Occasionally we
beheld a clear, sunny day, when heaven shone through and
all were invited to laugh with the joy of light. But those
eyes and those faces, those often hard-to-find smiles, made
up our world.

So, when the outside world touched down in the form
of a six-seater Piper twin-prop, it was like Christmas day,
heaven come to earth. Perhaps that's a bit of an overstate-
ment, but the anticipation of receiving a long-awaited care
package from home, or better yet, a visiting friend, easily

rivaled my childhood excitement for opening those gifts under the tree.

My mom became an expert bush-package-sender. She knew that without stores, fresh produce was almost impossible to come by once our initial supply from Anchorage ran out, so each year as she harvested her garden, she would meticulously cling-wrap, bubble-wrap, and newspaper-wrap her treasures: zucchini, carrots, cabbage, miniature watermelon, and even tomatoes. She would then seal them up in a Priority Mail Flat Rate box and send them north on a wing and a prayer.

About a week later I would start hovering near the VHF radio to listen for the airplane's call. I'd watch the weather, praying for the fog to roll out, cringing as the wind picked up intensity. I'd wait for my package to arrive. Sometimes, it would come within five days, and I'd call my mom as I opened the box, giving her a full report on how the produce survived. "One zucchini is broken, but edible ... looks like the container of tomatoes made it. Amazing!" Other times, nine, ten, twelve days would pass, and we would start to wonder if any of her garden greens would make it in any kind of usable condition. It was all a gamble. A game of waiting.

Over time, we discovered an organic produce company out of Seattle that we could order from bi-weekly, and although it cost a pretty penny, it was a predictable source of fresh delight. Better still was the day a sweet couple in Anchorage chose to be our "link" family. They linked us to all the resources of the big city, and all we had to do was email them our wish list every month and reimburse them the cost. Blessing of all blessings we didn't have to wait for our food to arrive from the Lower 48, so what they sent often came within a matter of days. But it was still dependent on the airplanes, which were dependent on the weather, which is dependent on God alone.

The worst was when we were the ones waiting for that plane, when our next three connecting flights depended on us getting out of the village that day. For the eight winter months of the year, we had to wear our cold-weather gear in order to fly. Safety regulations. So just in case you have a crash landing in the tundra or mountains you might not freeze to death before help arrives. Real comforting.

The day we were scheduled to leave we would have all our bags packed and by the door by 9:00 am. The planes didn't usually come that early; but if they were trying to beat a storm they might, so we had to be ready. We would hear word of the tentative schedule from the local agent, and that would usually give us a roughly trustworthy two-hour time frame in which to expect the airplane. But there had been times we'd been caught off-guard, so we'd learned to put on all our layers except our coat and hat and sit still while we waited so as not to overheat too much.

If the wind was gusting or the fog was heavy or the rain on the cusp of ice, we would pray that the airlines would have divine wisdom in whether it was safe to send a plane or not; and we would hope that if they did come, they would send Billy. Billy was the pilot renowned for landing safely in the most horrendous conditions. He was who the locals trusted most. Just please, God, don't let them send that new kid down today! We all knew that experience counted for a lot in the unpredictable conditions of Alaska Peninsula flying.

Most times, by the grace of God, we made it in or out when we had planned. But very rarely, we would sit at the gravel runway, expecting the plane to land within ten minutes, when we would hear the radio crackle. Conditions were worse than they expected. They would continue to the next village and pick us up on the return if the weather had improved. Our hearts would sink, and we would return to our house to wait some more.

In all the waiting, in all the unpredictability, I had no control. Worrying got me nowhere. I was utterly helpless, but not hopeless.

"God thunders with His voice wondrously,
Doing great things which we cannot comprehend.
For to the snow He says, 'Fall on the earth,'
And to the downpour and the rain, 'Be strong.'
He seals the hand of every man,
That all men may know His work.
Then the beast goes into its lair
And remains in its den.
Out of the south comes the storm,

And out of the north the cold.
From the breath of God ice is made,
And the expanse of the waters is frozen.
Also with moisture He loads the thick cloud;
He disperses the cloud of His lightning.
It changes direction, turning around by His guidance,
That it may do whatever He commands it
On the face of the inhabited earth.
Whether for correction, or for His world,
Or for lovingkindness, He causes it to happen."
JOB 37:5-13 NASB

Elihu counseled Job on the power of God in Job chapter 37. And God counseled me in His sovereignty in the myriad times of waiting for that plane—more round pen training. He alone held the whole picture in His hands, determining whether for correction, or for His world, or for lovingkindness, He would cause the wind to calm or the storm to rage.

Through the sleet and the sunshine, the disappointment and the rejoicing, the Creator forged in me a trust in His sovereignty that is the granite beneath my feet in every storm of life. A season of sickness or a season of health, He is at work, whether for correction or lovingkindness. A painful loss or an unexpected gift, He is behind it, whether for correction or lovingkindness. A traffic jam or three green lights in a row, He is setting the pace, whether for correction or for lovingkindness.

I say this not with a "whatever will be will be" passive attitude, but rather with a "whatever God wills surely happens" active hope. Because He is sovereign, not one word of His will return void, not one jot or tittle of His promises will remain unfulfilled, not one sparrow will fall to the ground apart from Him. And therefore, I can trust Him. In the waiting of the wilderness, trust is born.

Reflection Questions

What waiting experiences have taught you to trust God more deeply?

What is your response to the picture of an intentional, sovereign Creator in Job 37:5-13? The text quoted is in NASB. You might enjoy reading it in various translations.

Part 5

COLLISION

"We are so obsessed with doing that we have no time and no imagination left for being. As a result, men are valued not for what they are but for what they do or what they have—for their usefulness."

— Thomas Merton[1]

Comfortless

I FLOPPED TO MY LEFT side and plunked my head onto my pillow several times. Tucking the blanket over my ear, just how I like it, I breathed slowly and deeply, willing my body to relax into sleep. The baby inside me wouldn't have it. She punched and kicked as if trying to fluff her own bedding. After several minutes I readjusted my pillow and flipped my hair away from my neck. It didn't help. Nothing helped when Troy wasn't next to me.

Ugh. Maybe I should just get up and start all over again.

As I crossed the small kitchen on my way to the bathroom, I could see the light still on in Troy's classroom. He'd been there for hours already, creating another Science unit from scratch, or maybe he'd said he had Literature papers to grade. I couldn't remember. Probably both. And was it the end of October already? He must have end of month reports to submit, too. It was just always so much.

And I missed him.

I missed working alongside him. I missed regularly going to bed together. I missed being able to go out on a date. I missed *us*.

This new version of us was so busy doing our roles of mothering and teaching, that there was little time for anything else. The past three years had been full of growth in so many ways—our own children, our friendship with the Grossmanns, helping students achieve goals, developing a

185

healthy house-church—that we hardly noticed the diminishing of our own relationship. Oh, we still loved each other plenty, but we shared less laughter and fewer meaningful conversations. We shared less of the stuff that makes a relationship good, and more of the stuff that adds to its frustration.

But what could we do? There was work to be done here for God's kingdom; so we limped along, finding our enjoyment in the cute antics of our toddler, but rarely in each other.

It was an exact mirror of my relationship with God. But I wouldn't discover that until much later.

Setting my glass of water on the nightstand, I pulled back the comforter to my bed and crawled in. Snuggled into its downy warmth, I should have been comforted. Only I wasn't. I just wasn't.

Trying to get comfortable to sleep is one thing, but what about all the other creature comforts we seek after? As Christians, should we live for our own comfort? From a plush armchair, while reading on a shiny Kindle, with a five dollar macchiato in one hand and a view out the window to a new SUV, many of us will answer with a tongue-in-cheek "no." From an off-balance wooden bench, while reading a hand-me-down copy of this book, with a green tea in one hand and a view out the window to three people and a chicken puttering along on a motorcycle, some of us will answer with a firm, if not judgmental, "no."

Yet here we all are, lining our nests and our pockets to one degree or another so we can hopefully make it through this brutal world without too much pain and discomfort. We are awed and inspired by those who actually give more than ten percent to the church, those who devote their time and energy to discipleship and evangelism, those who uproot their family and learn a new language in order to share Christ with the unreached, those who choose to live in squalor so they can tangibly love the most impoverished people on the planet. Ooh. Aah. I could never do *that*, we say.

We make it all about what people have given up and the comforts they have knowingly spurned. And we see it as a great sacrifice.

Only it's not.

Jim Elliot, missionary martyr, says it well when he reminds us, "He is no fool who gives what he cannot keep to gain what he cannot lose."[1] And what is it that we gain for following Jesus through trials, suffering, and even death? Heaven, yes, and a pain-free, sorrow-free, separation-free eternity in the presence of the Lord God Almighty and the Lamb.[2] We are promised that we will see His face, and His name will be on our foreheads. Not only that, but we will reign forever and ever. It's like all our princess and superhero fantasies come true!

A glorious eternity is a strong motivator. But it takes a lot of faith and constant reminding to walk a life of obedience to Christ if we only have future promises to cling to.

We live in the here and now. We experience life, with all its pain and pleasure, in this temporal plane. That is the reality of our existence. And we don't want this earthly existence to be a miserable one. Of course not. We want to at least be like Paul, who confidently declares, "I have learned to be content whatever the circumstances. I know what it is to be in need, and I know what it is to have plenty. I have learned the secret of being content in any and every situation, whether well fed or hungry, whether living in plenty or in want" (Philippians 4:11-12). Oh Paul, do tell us this secret. We want to be content, too. And so, he simply shares this overquoted tidbit, "I can do everything through him who gives me strength" (Philippians 4:13).

Okay, I say. I have Jesus, so I have everything I need; and I should never be discontent. After all, I'm hardly starving or shipwrecked or left for dead. Surely I, too, can be content.

So, I hide my disappointment. I brush away my discomfort. I ignore the restless nights and the lackluster days. Because I just want to be a devoted, content Christian.

I hope you're seeing the problem here. Something critical is missing. Take a moment and ask yourself what's still lacking. If we have our eyes focused on eternity and our hearts filled with Jesus, is contentment with this meager life not enough?

I don't think my creative, boundless, triune God made me so I could merely be content. No, His ravishing, extravagant glory is shown when I live in joy. Abundant, exuberant joy.

The words "joy" and "rejoice" show up in the NIV Bible over 400 times. Oftentimes, we are commanded to rejoice. In fact, just before his statement about contentment, Paul tells the Philippians, "Rejoice in the Lord always. I will say it again: Rejoice!" (4:4). Paul may have known the secret to contentment, but more importantly, he knew the treasure of joy.

Contentment, I have learned, is often a byproduct of gratitude. It can be contrived by giving thanks. But joy, it would seem, is a deeper response, an almost uncontainable emotion. It reveals itself in squeals of delight, spontaneous dancing, giggles, clapping, and tears. Like a child leaping into the arms of a grandparent they haven't seen for months, or a bride unable to subdue her smile as she walks the aisle to her beloved, joy is mesmerizing, enrapturing, and irrepressible.

Joy comes from the heart of God.

Why else would He create the lily with such a tantalizing fragrance and a wide-open face of beauty, or the platypus with its humorous blend of duck and beaver features? Why would yawns be contagious and kisses a universal token of affection? Why would the sky catch fire at dawn and dusk and the moon grin at us with his silvery face? Why would ducklings be downy, cats purr, and horses be swift and sleek? Why would strawberries bleed with a juicy sweetness and lemons make us pucker? God created all these for our joy. And we are created to enjoy. While seeking our own earthly comforts might stifle our relationship with Christ, seeking our own joy in His presence and the good gifts He gives will always draw us closer. If I might make a bold statement, I would dare to say that if we are not living in joy, we are not living in the rhythm of the Giver's heart. For in Him, there is fullness of joy. Not that we won't be sad, or we won't grieve, or we won't ever face heartache or even clinical depression; but that even in those times, when we pause and reach out to the Father, we can still touch, taste, and feel His joy. It's part of the living water within, fed from the never-ending stream of the Spirit.

Therefore, ignoring my irritants in an effort to gain contentment, might be pushing me farther away from God's design for me. However, acknowledging the pains—no matter how trite they might seem—can help me release them to the Father and create sacred space inside for His joy. But acknowledging the pain means facing it. It means calling it what it is, admitting I've been sweeping it under the rug, seeking reconciliation where needed, and releasing my need to hold on to it.

My capacity to acknowledge and feel pain seems to be directly linked to my capacity for joy. It's like they're two sides of the same coin—at least while we traipse this planet in its sin-broken state. Someday, on a new earth, we will know joy sans pain; but for now, they're wed. To ignore one is to ignore the other. As I keep walking this mysterious journey of faith, I discover that even pain, discomfort, and irritation can be a gift. God uses them to show me where He is working, where I am resisting Him, and where He wants to do something new. And oh, there are so many beautiful things He wants to make new in my life. But He cannot do that if I don't admit they need remaking or that the change has to start with me. My heart. My pain. My joy. Not the circumstances. Not the other person. Me.

That night, as I tossed and turned, vainly attempting to subdue my body and mind, I began to realize I was up against a wall and something needed to change. The only problem was, I refused to believe it was me. I had denied myself certain comforts for the sake of Christ's kingdom, and I believed I was all the more devout for it; but somewhere along the way, I had also begun denying myself both the joy and the pain of being fully alive in Christ. Stay busy. Stay focused. Stay content. That's what kept me going—or so I thought.

Have you ever faced a time in a relationship where you shared less of the stuff that brings joy and more of the stuff that adds frustration? How did you navigate this?

In what ways do you hide your disappointment and restlessness out of a desire to just be a devoted, content Christian?

Do you agree that there is a direct link between the full experience of joy to the full experience of pain? How has this played out in your life?

All the Reasons

WE'D BEEN HAVING THIS CONVERSATION for a while now. The one where we talked about all the reasons to go; all the reasons to stay. It seemed there were one hundred reasons for both, rendering neither side inherently better than the other. But despite the discussions, the prayers, the lists, and the inquiries, my mind was already made up. This would be our last year in Alaska.

At seven years in, with college loans paid off and experience under our belts, there was a world of teaching possibilities open to us. Literally. And although we were already living among the unreached and underprivileged right where we were, we never had shaken the desire to do so in a foreign nation—a country that was dominated by a different religion. Who's to say if it was more of a stirring of the Spirit or a resurrection of the old savior complex? Either way, the draw to teach and serve overseas still tugged on us like a magnet.

Besides, Wade would be graduating in a few months, and we didn't have a close discipleship connection with any of the other high schoolers. The school itself had barely been hanging on, scrounging up an extra relative or two to visit each October for the last two years to make sure we had the minimum of ten students enrolled during the "count period." Even Matthew and Rachel had talked about

193

moving somewhere else with a more predictable student population.

Then there was the new field our mission organization was opening in Southeast Asia. After asking some questions and doing some online digging, we had discovered an incredible international school in Northern Thailand whose vision arrested our hearts: Serve the Servants. Yes and amen to that. We knew full well how challenging cross-cultural ministry work could be, and we knew how exhausting it was to serve without support; so being part of providing a safe, quality education for the kids of these servant families so they could continue to do their pastoral training, anti-trafficking, hilltribe evangelizing, orphan loving, church planting, resource developing work was a privilege. Not only that, but thirty percent of the students at this school came from Buddhist families who just wanted their children to have an English education. They would certainly get that, along with a whole heap of Jesus through Bible classes, weekly chapel, and teachers who could talk about God freely.

It was perfect. It all lined up. And it was an easy sell, not only to us, but also to everyone who asked. We were moving onward and upward in terms of how the Church views missions.

We didn't have to do any explaining—least of all to ourselves—of why we were so relieved to be leaving Alaska. We didn't have to face the fact that maybe, just maybe, we were running away from something. We didn't have to revisit the trauma of our first three years in the bush and consider the ways we were still haunted by it.

What we *did* have was a three-year old boy, a brand-new baby, and two months between leaving Alaska and flying to Thailand. As I write that out, I realize it sounds absolutely insane. But I think the other option—staying indefinitely in Alaska—felt even more insane at the time.

I remember one very revealing conversation with Rachel that went something like this:

"I'm just really looking forward to a big school where Troy only has to teach a couple of subjects. Not *all* of them. And he won't have all that tedious paperwork that goes with the Head Teacher role. I mean, he'll probably still coach basketball, but he should have a lot more time, which will be so nice."

Rachel studied me for a moment while sipping her tea. "Yeah, I hope so. But, he's still gonna be Troy, you know? He just likes to be involved in everything. Changing places doesn't change a person," she said with a knowing laugh.

I shrugged. "I know, but I really think a fresh start will be good for us." I watched out the window as a flock of ptarmigan lit out of the bushes across the pond. I sighed. "*Something* has to change."

It's shocking to me how natural self-deception is. How easy it is to fall into. How incredibly hard it is to uncover. We find a good, believable reason to explain an action to someone else; and before we know it, we believe it too.

Perhaps it's because we truly are always a mixed soup of motives. A few potatoes for Jesus, some carrots for the church, a bit of beef for me, and a dash of pepper for whoever else might be affected by my decision. It's easy to emphasize one reason over another to flavor our story.

I wasn't *trying* to tell people only the positive reasons for moving to Thailand while omitting the negative reasons we wanted to leave Alaska; I just truly convinced myself that those *were* the main reasons. Oh, I knew we were tired, but I certainly wouldn't have admitted we were edging on burnout. I knew I wanted to push a reset button for the way we balanced family and school, but I didn't understand that what I needed was a full reset on my relationship with God and how I viewed all of our roles and responsibilities. It's just plain hard to see what we don't want to see.

Those people in our lives, the Rachels, who can see into us more clearly than we can see into ourselves, are more than just good friends. They can be life savers. They can help us take a good, hard look at our life in the moment, and they can warn us of the pitfalls ahead that our self-deception is blind to. A friend like that isn't easy to come by, mostly because we must be intentional and trusting enough to let someone get so close that they can see the difference between what's really going on and what we present on the outside.

And we are a presentation culture, aren't we? Social media, of course, is infamous for spurring on the desire to show off our best side while omitting the rest.

Unfortunately, it seems to happen in the church frequently, too. Put on your Sunday best, train the kids to sit still and behave, listen to a well-rehearsed worship set and a clear three-point sermon. We don't leave a lot of room for showing our weakness, or wrestling through tough issues or decisions together, or even genuine confession and repentance. It would seem that the desire to wear a mask and fit the mold is a part of our sin-nature that creeps into just about everything. Even our relationship with God.

How ironic that with the one person who knows us better than we know ourselves, we attempt to put on a show. But not for the sake of impressing Him. Most of us know better than that. We say our "powerful" prayers and sing our "heartfelt" songs because we want Him to love us. Ultimately, that's why we do any of our performing for people, as well. We just want to be loved.

But what if I told you that you would be loved just the same if you never prayed another coherent prayer? Never sang another worship song? Never read another scripture? Never fed another hungry mouth? Never raised another dollar? Never taught another child? Never wrote another word?

If you were physically and mentally incapacitated tonight, would you still be lovable? More than that, would the love of our extravagant God still pursue you? Did Jesus Christ die for the invalid with as much passionate hope of restoring their relationship as he had when he died for (insert your most inspirational hero of the faith here)?

Ah, it's easy to answer "yes" from our heads, but hard to live out that "yes" with our hearts and lives. We want to prove our worth; but of all the reasons that Christ died for you, your productivity and presentation were not among them. Jesus flips our value system on its head with this parable:

> "For the kingdom of heaven is like a landowner who went out early in the morning to hire workers for his vineyard. He agreed to pay them a denarius for the day and sent them into his vineyard.
>
> About nine in the morning he went out and saw others standing in the marketplace doing nothing. He told them, "You also go and work in my vineyard, and I will pay you whatever is right." So they went.
>
> He went out again about noon and about three in the afternoon and did the same thing. About five in the afternoon he went out and found still others standing around. He asked them, "Why have you been standing here all day long doing nothing?"
>
> "Because no one has hired us," they answered.
>
> He said to them, "You also go and work in my vineyard."
>
> When evening came, the owner of the vineyard said to his foreman, "Call the workers and pay them their wages, beginning with the last ones hired and going on to the first."

The workers who were hired about five in the afternoon came and each received a denarius. So when those came who were hired first, they expected to receive more. But each one of them also received a denarius. When they received it, they began to grumble against the landowner. "These who were hired last worked only one hour," they said, "and you have made them equal to us who have borne the burden of the work and the heat of the day." But he answered one of them, "I am not being unfair to you, friend. Didn't you agree to work for a denarius? Take your pay and go. I want to give the one who was hired last the same as I gave you. Don't I have the right to do what I want with my own money? Or are you envious because I am generous?" So the last will be first, and the first will be last."

MATTHEW 20:1-16

Parents and teachers know that "that's not fair" is the worst argument ever. Apparently, God thinks so too. What's not fair is that any of us bums get invited to work in His vineyard. It's terribly unfair that we wayward street rats are allowed into the wedding supper of the Lamb (Matthew 22:1-14). The fact that my Creator and King died in my place is impossibly unfair. No, none of us are worthy of any of these unfair gifts of grace. And we never will be. The more highly I exalt His unmerited grace, the more readily I cast aside my pathetic performance to please Him and earn His love. I can't earn what is already mine.

But then, in light of His lavish grace, I want to love Him in return. My motive has changed from striving to gratitude, but I am still doing all the same things with the same religious fervor. We often hear the call to love Jesus through our obedience, but we forget that the greatest command we are to obey is to simply love (John 15:10-12). The words of God, the jealous husband, in Hosea 6:6 pierce deep, especially in The Living Bible translation: "I don't want your sacrifices—I want your love; I don't want your offerings—I want you to know me."

This God, who has always been and forever will be after our hearts before anything else, sees right through our motives and all the reasons we have to do this, move there, stop that, and start this. He knows we want His love. He knows we're grateful for all He's done. He knows we're blinded by the dust we kick up in our own scampering back and forth to serve Him. He knows it all, and He draws us nearer still.

And in those rare moments that we sit down with Him over a cup of tea and have a bit of an honest conversation, we just might hear Him say, "You know, changing places won't change you. Only my presence can do that. So why don't you just sit with me a while longer, and tell me more about what's really going on?"

Reflection Questions

Think about the friends who have helped you see your own soul more clearly. Thank God for them and consider how you can be the same kind of wise listener.

Ask the Lord to reveal one way you are self-deceived right now. What's your greatest blind spot? (Hint: It's quite possibly connected to what you think you need most.)

Do your actions show that you think God wants your sacrifices more or your love more?

The Painful Beautiful

AND JUST LIKE THAT, FOUR years in our second village were behind us. We'd sold most of our stuff, Troy had a position promised at a school in northern Thailand, and we were pathetically attempting to prepare our hearts for the goodbyes that were racing toward us.

Parting ways with our families when we went to college across the country was difficult, and leaving behind friends and a beloved church when we left Minnesota for Alaska was sad. But this. This saying goodbye to a place where we had found redemption from the difficulties of our first stint in the village, and especially saying goodbye to the people whom we would not have survived without, was like ripping apart two pieces of paper that had been glued together. You can't do it without inevitable tearing.

We knew this season was closing by God's hand, but we didn't know how to separate gracefully from the Grossmanns. Rachel and I were a lifeline for each other in motherhood; taking each other's children when we needed to get something done or just have a break, supplying one another with dinner inspiration from our never-changing pantries, and just being that sister-friend that is always there to laugh or cry with. We knew each other, our spouses, and our children better than anyone outside of family probably ever will. You can't live right next to someone in an isolated village, facing the same struggles and joys together, without developing an incredibly tight bond, especially when the Spirit of God is between you, giving grace to forgive and love one another in spite of our shortcomings.

Matthew and Rachel were going through their own transition grief as they had been in the village for six total years and were also preparing to move on, feeling that they needed to be in a place of greater spiritual support now that we were leaving. Matthew got a job in a different village that had an established church and Bible camp; and while we were all excited about what was next, we still had to face the reality of the dramatic change that was about to happen to our relationship.

So, we tried to hold on to the treasure of the four years we had with the Grossmanns with a thankful heart and also let ourselves grieve the goodbye. I'm not sure we did so well, being caught up in the whirlwind of the transition and the busyness of preparing for life overseas; but deep down we did know that the pain of this goodbye was only there because of the beauty of our "hello, let's be friends."

The picture of our runway send-off from the village still hangs above my computer. Troy and I are surrounded by six children of various sizes. A tiny baby Rinnah is strapped to my chest and the wind is whipping my shoulder-length hair back. Rachel stands next to me holding Chanan. We're all smiling, like we're taking a photo after a great day at the beach. But really those smiles were holding back the tears. We were letting go of those kids, placing them in the Father's care, unsure if anyone else would come along to teach them more about Jesus. We were moving on; they were staying put. They had welcomed us and trusted us, and now we were leaving them. It did not feel good.

We travelled with Matthew, Rachel, Malachi, and little Caleb as far as Anchorage, where we lingered longer than we probably should have, letting the boys play just one minute more before heading to our separate gates. And separate lives. If we'd been "married" for four years, then this was the "divorce." Finally, one of us said it—it was probably Rachel since she was always the best at moving people the direction they needed to go— "Well, we'd better get this over with." And then the long hugs. Tears watching the boys who thought they were brothers hug playfully, clueless to the significance of this goodbye. One more quick hug. And then the parting. The walking away, step by step abandoning the dearest friendship I'd ever known.

Yes, we would see each other again. Yes, we have the internet and can still talk. But never again would we jog down the boardwalk to the other's house, bursting in the door with a child on the hip and a flurry of snow at our backs. Never again would we kneel side by side in the squishy tundra, picking berries and talking about children and dinner and life. Never again would we throw a birthday party for the other, making polka dot cheesecake or dark chocolate ganache. We chose to let all that go. Again, it did not feel good.

And yet, I thought I was more than ready to move on. That change I was so eager for was on the horizon. We were headed for a tropical adventure and a chance to start over. This was what I wanted. Wasn't it?

I'm reminded, as I sit here at 1:00 AM because I can't sleep and just have to put these words on paper, that God gives me incredibly beautiful gifts in every situation. It is an utter tragedy to overlook them because I want a way out of the challenges surrounding them.

One of the keys to unlocking His joy in any and every situation is to rejoice in the treasures He gives. It would seem, however, that some of His treasures are buried. They might be hidden beneath our unmet expectations and have years of disappointment and heartache piled on top. But they are there. Like one patiently panning for gold, we must take a good scoop of the slurry of our lives and sift through it, letting God rinse away the silt and muck to reveal the shining nuggets.

One of the curiosities about humans is that we often don't appreciate something until it's gone. Electricity, water, health, phones, fresh air, a job, and even friendships are all so easily taken for granted. More than that, we complain about these things when they aren't working perfectly. *Ugh, my internet keeps cutting out. This job is so boring. I sure wish I could lose just ten more pounds. Geez, the sun is so bright.* Aren't we funny? Ridiculous, even.

It's easy to scoff when we read the accounts of the Israelites grumbling as they made their way to the Promised Land, forgetting how closely it resembles our own lives. Numbers 21:4-5 details one of their more vehement displays of frustration:

> "They traveled from Mount Hor along the route to the Red Sea, to go around Edom. But the people grew impatient on the way; they spoke against God and against Moses, and said, 'Why have you brought us up out of Egypt to die in the desert? There is no bread! There is no water! And we detest this miserable food!'"

I read that and almost roll my eyes. How could they be so callous to the miraculous provision of manna? How could they think that life as an overworked slave in Egypt could possibly be better? How could they speak against the God who revealed Himself so clearly and powerfully through countless miracles right before their eyes? In fact, just one chapter prior we read the account of God bringing water out of a rock to quench their thirst. Surely, they should have been inclined to ask this Great Provider for what they needed instead of grumbling against Him. But that was not their go-to response; and neither is it ours.

God's reaction to their childish outburst is equally shocking. He sends venomous snakes among them. After people start dying from the snake bites, the Israelites confess that they have sinned and ask Moses to pray for the snakes to go away. Interestingly, when Moses prays, the Lord doesn't remove the snakes; but He does give directions for a cure. Moses is to make a bronze snake and put it on a pole so that when the people look at it after they've been bitten, they will live (Numbers 21:6-9).

It's as if the Israelites had been bitten by a viper called Lack of Faith, and they didn't believe that God would provide for their needs or lead them down the right path. They didn't believe He was good. The poison of mistrust coursed through their veins. And it's not God's way to do an unsolicited blood transfusion; rather, He provides the antivenin of Faith. The people had intentionally acted against God, now they must intentionally look toward Him. They must set their eyes and their trust on this figure, lifted up on a pole. The only way to be saved from death was a simple act of faith.

Thousands of years later, a diligent student of the Torah who would have known this story well, sits before Jesus one night, wondering if he can trust this new, miracle working teacher. Jesus challenges Nicodemus to take a leap of faith, stating that, "just as Moses lifted up the snake in the desert, so the Son of Man must be lifted up, that everyone who believes in him may have eternal life" (John 3:14-15).

So, the question that we, the Israelites, and Nicodemus are faced with is, "Will you believe?" Will you believe that He is good? That His goodness is enough to save you? That He gives you good gifts, even in the misery of your wilderness?

When we look to Him in faith rather than frustration, we find that His fingerprints have been all over our story; and they have left a residue of goodness every place they have touched. We are surprised to discover that it doesn't matter how many miracles we have or have not personally witnessed. Our grumbling and our doubting and our clamoring for a change is only stilled by a simple act of faith. We turn our eyes upon Jesus, and the things of earth grow strangely dim. And then, only then, can we clearly see the miraculous treasures that He has already tucked in every corner of our lives... A stranger's smile that we needed when we didn't even realize we were feeling down. A gentle breeze on a sweltering day. A ten-dollar bill in the pants you wore but didn't wash last week. The exact right song at the exact right moment on your shuffled playlist. A phone call or a message from a friend just because they were thinking of you. A heart wrenching goodbye that reminds you how deeply you have been privileged to love.

These gifts signify the treasures of His goodness that just seem to fall out of His pockets wherever He goes. They are the evidence of the presence of the Omnipresent One.

Reflection Questions

What has God asked you to let go of that is both painful and beautiful in its release?

How do you respond to these questions posed in the text?
Will you believe that He is good?
That His goodness is enough to save you?
That He gives you good gifts, even in the misery of your wilderness?

Ask the Lord to reveal some "buried treasure" gifts in your situation right now that you haven't appreciated.

Upside Down and Backward

I PUSHED MY ORANGE STROLLER, the one I had broken in on the gravel roads of rural Alaska, over a lilting chunk of concrete protruding from what could almost be called a sidewalk. This time, a baby girl was tucked inside, her bare, white toes wiggling as we entered the market. A torn-eared dog stared at us from under a table loaded with knobby, green pumpkins. Rubber boots, mounds of curry paste, and unidentifiable meat on a stick were among the food and wares available to buy.

"Wook, Mama!" Chanan exclaimed, bounding ahead to a tub on the ground. Slimy snake-like creatures writhed inside.

Keenly aware that we were being watched, I repressed the feeling of disgust that tried to escape through my expression and smiled instead. "Yep. Those are eels. I think." I wasn't sure I knew what anything was anymore.

"Oooh, fwoggies! They're so big." The next tub awed him with its toads, and the one after that with its catfish.

In our brief pause, several vendors came out from behind their tables and were talking to six-month old Rinnah.

"Jah-aye!" they cooed, playing the timeless game of peek-a-boo with her. One woman touched her bare toes and frowned, then caressed her wispy blonde hair and rattled off a stream of syllables to me that seemed friendly enough, although I understood nothing. I awkwardly clapped my hands together in front of my face and bowed a bit too low, attempting to politely excuse myself from their scrutiny. We turned a corner away from the flapping, splashing fish and found an aisle that looked promising. A table of vegetables I mostly recognized enticed me. I grabbed some carrots, cucumbers, onions and tomatoes then handed them to the vendor to be weighed as I had watched my neighbor do a few days prior. She told me the price. Apparently, the studying of numbers I had been doing wasn't going to help me decipher her Northern Thai dialect just yet. I handed her a bill, hoping it was enough, and received a surprising amount of change in return.

After passing a table with flowers and candles, I found a fruit stand. We loaded up on watermelon, pineapple, mango, those funny, fuzzy rambutan fruit I had just been introduced to, and a kilo of my new favorite—mangosteen. I studied the signs designating the price, trying to recognize any of the Thai characters I had learned. Yes, that looked like the "chicken" one that made the "g" sound! I internally applauded myself.

Our trek home from the market was less than half a mile, but storm clouds were brewing, and I knew they could let loose with a tropical downpour at any moment. I had Chanan hop on the footrest at the front of the stroller, stuffed our fresh produce into the pouch underneath the seat, and set my weight into pushing my load home. I crossed over to the right side of the road so we could move with the flow of traffic, but after getting buzzed by an oncoming motorcycle I realized my mistake. Traffic drives on the left here.

In fact, everything seemed to be opposite from what I had grown up with. Tones in the language express entirely different words, not feelings; writing not only uses unique characters, but it also has no spaces or punctuation; the economy is cash-based with few places that accept cards; everything is metric; the steering wheel is on the right, not the left, and the stick shift is on the left, not the right; toilets were often seatless, leaving one to squat over a hole that at least had a ceramic bowl but never toilet paper; and even our days were upside down, being fifteen hours ahead of the US Pacific time zone we flew out of.

Yes, we were on a brand-new adventure, for sure. We spent our first year in Thailand exploring the street markets, making new friends, teaching Chanan to ride a bicycle and Rinnah to walk, figuring out the currency exchange and exactly how much we needed to live off of, and battling the cockroaches and spiders that seemed to come out of all the cracks in our concrete house. Troy ended up teaching more classes than originally planned plus taking on the role of student council advisor. There was plenty to keep us distracted and very little reason for us to look back.

We threw ourselves headlong into our new lives, determined to uncover the intricacies of life in Thailand while figuring out how to *not* accidentally order chicken foot soup… again. It was both hilarious and exhausting, and for the most part we were just incredibly grateful to be so close to fresh food year-round that we didn't care if we weren't always sure exactly what we were eating. We were also thrilled to be part of a larger missionary community and to have multiple friends that lived in our neighborhood. It felt like we'd gone from famine to feast in several ways. Life was fascinating and meaningful and very, very different.

Reflection Questions

How do you find yourself responding to this abrupt change of continents and lifestyle? Have you ever had a similar upheaval of your own doing?

Are you in a season of life that keeps you distracted and busy and prevents you from doing the intentional soul work of looking back with God's eyes on your hurts from the previous season? How can you create margin for the healing to begin?

Never Enough

IF OUR FIRST YEAR IS a crisp capture of those thrilling moments of discovery, our second year is a blurry streak. The highlights are there—moving into a newer house, helping organize a weekly playgroup with some neighbors who also had preschoolers at home, and having my mom visit around Christmastime. But I can't give flesh to the memories of daily life.

Daily life was simply surviving motherhood with an intense four-year old and a two-year old who decided naps were already a thing of the past. Daily life was meal after meal with just me and the kids. Daily life was managing the shopping trips and keeping the budget and desperately clinging to the rare, undistracted moments I had with my husband.

I think I remember so little of daily life from that year because I have memory loss from banging my head against a figurative wall. Daily life was the grind, not the glamour, of missions. And I just kept soldiering on, ignoring the blood dripping down my forehead.

That second year, the school's principal took a (well-earned and wisely chosen) sabbatical. Troy, with his Head Teacher experience from Alaska, was asked to fill this role. At the same time, the woman who had been overseeing the technology department announced she wouldn't be returning until the second semester; and Troy, with his somewhat

COLLIDING WITH THE CALL

sufficient knowledge of computers, took on her position, as well. Then, the Athletic Director had a family emergency that pulled him back to the States for a while. You can guess who stepped in.

All this while continuing his teaching and coaching roles, plus occasionally preaching at the bilingual church we attended, and helping at the Bible study of a friend's ministry to the Shan people an hour north of us.

Troy didn't sleep much that year, but he got it all done. Held it all together. I didn't laugh much that year, but I kept the children alive. Held it all together. We were serving the servants, after all. Doing what God had called us to do. Pouring out our lives as an offering to our King. Forsaking worldly comfort for His name's sake.

It sounds noble, doesn't it? It sounds like a hard-working missionary family that is doing a lot of good, and therefore must be worthy of your support.

Or maybe it sounds ignorant, prideful, Pharisaical even. I don't know. What I do know is that the joy in our marriage plummeted even lower that year. And I knew we couldn't keep going at that pace, but I didn't know how to change. Troy and I would have circular conversations about it all, never finding solid footing to step forward on. I felt betrayed by his busyness. He felt mistrusted by my constant questioning of his decisions. We both felt hopeless.

If only the kids slept better …

If only we had family nearby so dates were easier …

216

If only coworkers could stick around and do their jobs consistently ...

If only the school had a few more teachers to share the load ...

If only we had a bit more financial support ...

If only God would speak more clearly ...

If only ...

It seemed there was never enough time, or energy, or people, or resources, or attention to go around. Our lives were incredibly full while our souls were desperately impoverished.

Years before, I must have been paying at least a bit of attention in my economics class, because recently the phrase "scarcity versus abundance mentality" resurged from my memory. If you do an internet search on it, you'll find a lot of interesting articles on getting out of debt, succeeding in the business world, and understanding the psychological underpinnings of the poor. But God didn't bring it to mind so I could create more financial security in my life. He used it to show me the concrete shift that has happened in my spirit since that second year in Thailand.

It was a change in my thinking that crept in slowly and retreated slowly, all without my awareness. Until God opened my eyes to it in hindsight.

Scarcity can be both real and imagined. During that second year I *didn't* have very much emotional or relational support. We *were* underfunded. Troy and I *did* walk around

217

sleep deprived most days. There was an actual scarcity of some pretty basic needs in our lives. And that messes with your mind. Amid the place of actual lack, the brain decides it needs to focus on clinging and collecting, grasping and gathering, so you can somehow have enough to survive. Your focus tends toward supplying the need rather than gratitude, generosity, or rejoicing.

Unfortunately, even when the time of scarcity has passed, your brain can stay stuck in the mode of hoarding rather than appreciating the now-sufficient supply. So, what was the one thing I felt most dependent on and least able to access? Time with my husband. I became resentful and jealous of the things and people that would take him away from me. And yet even when I did get time, when he would give up a casual basketball game to stay home with me on a Friday night, I couldn't really appreciate or enjoy him. It still wasn't enough.

Whew. Poor man. He really is the rock of the two of us. Even amid my controlling ways, he just kept giving and loving and sacrificing. Trying to meet my needs, fill my emotionally starving belly, assuage my constant fears. The only problem was, no human is meant to entirely satisfy the longings of another. There is only One who can do that.

One who promises abundant life. One who guides us to the still waters, restores our souls, and prepares a banquet for us right before our enemy called Scarcity[1]. But how I learned to lean into the One who can satisfy is another story, another book. For now, suffice it to say that knowing

Christ and all His promises is never enough, either. It's not about the knowing, it's about the experiencing. There are many things we can grasp for, but only one thing we can really grasp onto because it is already grasping us: the all-consuming love of God.

So, I pray this for you, dear reader, and still for myself, too, because we all need to know what surpasses knowledge:

"For this reason, I kneel before the Father, from whom every family in heaven and on earth derives its name. I pray that out of his glorious riches he may strengthen you with power through his Spirit in your inner being, so that Christ may dwell in your hearts through faith. And I pray that you, being rooted and established in love, may have power, together with all the Lord's holy people, to grasp how wide and long and high and deep is the love of Christ, and to know this love that surpasses knowledge—that you may be filled to the measure of all the fullness of God.

Now to him who is able to do immeasurably more than all we ask or imagine, according to his power that is at work within us, to him be glory in the church and in Christ Jesus throughout all generations, forever and ever! Amen."

EPHESIANS 3:14-21

Now that's life-changing, mind-altering abundance. Go on back and pray it for yourself again. This time for your family. And again for your congregation or students or disciples or friends. Pray it on your knees, like Paul. Pray it out loud. Pray it until you believe it. And then pray it again. May the fullness of God fill you and transform you. Amen.

Reflection Questions

What are your "if only..." statements?

What do those statements reveal about your trust in the Lord as well as the focus of your heart?

Really take time to pray Ephesians 3:14-21 over yourself and your loved ones. Ask for a shift in your mindset so you can move away from scarcity and into His abundance.

He Found Me

I LAID DOWN ON THE rock-hard hotel bed, eager for a nap. Just an hour or so of rest before helping with the evening activities at the Women's Retreat should refresh me. I loved being part of the planning team for these events, but it could be tiring. And this year I was the emcee, so I really needed to be on top of all the details and scheduling.

My roommate, a sweet gal I was acquainted with from church, would spend her free time by the pool. I could just enjoy the solitude. "Thank you, Father, for a bit of sleep," I prayed as I closed my eyes.

As I lay there in the silence, sleep wouldn't come, but something else entirely unexpected came. It bubbled to the surface from a deep, aching space within. It shouted from the void inside. As a sharp sense of loneliness overtook me, I drenched my pillow with my tears. My body shook with sorrow as years of missing family support, longing for a friendship like I had with Rachel, and desiring joy and laughter in my marriage again were squeezed out of my heart. Those were things I preferred not to think about, things I hoped would just resolve themselves with time. Why was I crying about them now?

But I couldn't shake it. The dam had cracked and now all that loneliness poured out in one big, ugly cry. When was the last time I had even cried? I couldn't remember.

Finally, tears spent, I mopped my face and sat down to journal. I didn't really know what to say, but as I wrote I realized—as I so often do when my heart can express its words through pen and paper—that God was speaking to me. He found me in my one moment of stillness. For all my scampering and serving to make this weekend beautiful for other women, God had been patiently waiting for me to give Him space to love on me, too. And that's what these tears were, a gift of love. Having a word for some of the sadness I felt was a gift, too. I was lonely. Surrounded by hundreds of "friends" and yet still relatively unknown. I didn't have the remedy or even the next step, I only had one word: lonely.

But in that word, I was reminded of two things. One, if God brought it to the surface it must be for a reason. My hope was stirred that He didn't want me to stay in this place of loneliness. And, two, God had found me. I may have been busy and tired and not even seeking after Him, but He was seeking after me.

He is always seeking after me.

That our perfect, self-sustaining, galaxy-making God would pursue me, his sin-broken, trifling with the world, desperately needy daughter, leaves me incredulous. I will never pretend to understand it. He doesn't merely invite us in, He stands at the door and knocks (Revelation 3:20). He doesn't only welcome us when we return, He honors us with a party and celebrates us with His best (Luke 15:22-24). Ours is a God who chases after our hearts. Does He win us over because He is love and it's simply in His nature? I suppose so. Does He hunt us down because it brings Him greater glory as He magnifies His goodness? I believe so. Does He ensnare our affections because our joy, in some unquantifiable way, brings Him joy? I think it's possible. But I really don't know. I only know that, like the helpless beggar, I once was blind; but now I see. And not because I found Him—I couldn't have even if I wanted to. Only because He found me.

It's mercy beyond mercy.

And God's pursuit of us is incredibly personal. Yes, He loves all His children, even the lost ones, universally. But He also finds me and loves me specifically. He loves you specifically, too.

As Jesus walked through Galilee, He found His disciples and He called them to follow. They were fishing. Sitting under a tree. Collecting taxes. Going about the humdrum of their everyday lives with little thought to seeking out a teacher, a savior. But then He appeared in their lives one day, and with a word or a gesture or perhaps for some just a smile, He beckoned. And before He even had the renown of a miracle-worker, they were compelled by the Spirit to follow Him. It looked like a mid-life crisis on their part and a desperate collecting of friends, regardless of their reputations, on His part. It appeared random, abrupt, and nonsensical. But it was the wisdom of God that so often looks like foolishness to men.

That same nonsensical yet impeccable wisdom of God chose you. Chose me.

I know I'm talking theology here. Predestination and free will and all that. So, if you adamantly disagree then go ahead and laugh at me. That's your choice. Your exercise of free will. But I'm convinced that I would not belong to God if He had not already chosen me, pursued me, and awakened me with His Spirit. And yes, allowed me to choose Him back. Jesus does say that He stands at the door and knocks. He doesn't break it down or pick the lock. He allows us our doors and our pigpens and our wanderings. But when you're a lost sheep, tangled in the brambles with night falling and jackals howling, the sight of that Shepherd—who left all the rest to find you—is awfully appealing. Irresistible even.

You may not be running from God, but I imagine that in one way or another you are hiding. Like I was. Like Adam and Eve were. We can't help but retreat into our shame—perhaps over a sin, or perhaps over a general feeling of disappointment. Like my loneliness, we tend to take our weaknesses and bury them. It's a classic toddler ploy. If I can't see it, it must be gone. We can cover up our shame and our pain with all the good things we are doing and all the right sermonettes. We can shove it down so deep beneath our desire to serve and to keep up the appearance of ministry success that even we forget it's there.

But all the hurt and disappointment and frustration *is* still there. If it were up to us, it would just stay hidden, contained behind a tidy wall. This wall, white-washed and shiny on the outside, would keep people from digging around where we don't want them. We think it keeps them and us safe from our messes, our mistakes, our fragility. We think we need those broken shards of our dreams to stay tucked away where they can't cut us anymore. We probably even think it's what Jesus would want us to do— just pick up our cross and carry on. But our walls do more to trap us than to protect us.

When El Roi, the God Who Sees, nudges something hidden to the surface, it's because He wants to set you free. He wants to call your hurt, your sin, and your shame out into the light. He wants to peel back the defenses and pretenses of all your good works, and just hold you close as you stare together at The Big Ugly that you've been shoving back into a closet whenever it peeks out. He wants to help you name it, because once you name something you own it. You master it, and it no longer masters and manipulates you. He doesn't ask you to fight it or heal it on your own; He only asks you to expose it and surrender it.

It might sound horrifying and painful, but it's like major surgery that will save your life. Nobody wants to be cut open, but it sure beats letting the cancer continue to grow. God only wants to expose the places He wants to heal. Patiently, He will pursue you. Every part of you. He asks for total surrender, even of the loneliness, the anxiety, the

exhaustion, and the desperation. So, what's your Big Ugly?
What is the Holy Spirit waiting to help you uncover and
release? It's getting dark and the jackals are coming. Your
wall is a useless illusion. Let the Good Shepherd find you
and   bring   you   home.

Reflection   Questions

When has a moment of stillness, planned or unplanned, allowed space for the Lord to speak directly to your heart?

Do you think of God as seeking after you? Can you think
of a time you recognized you were pursued by the Spirit?

What "Big Ugly" is God inviting you to shove into the light
so it will no longer remain a hidden master?

Undivided

MY PROTECTIVE WALL NOW HAD a fissure called Loneliness. And I didn't care for it at all. I wanted it patched, filled, satisfied. I didn't want my defenses to crumble. I didn't want my good sense to cave way. I didn't mean to giggle a little too often and check the mirror a second time. I didn't mean to let my thoughts stampede out of control and my heart grow attached. I didn't realize it was anything. Until it was already a something.

All I knew was that it felt really good to laugh again. It felt gratifying to be noticed and appreciated, even in the smallest ways. It felt natural to replay the fun moments we had together over and over in my mind. I had all the symptoms of an infatuation—a childish crush. And he had no idea. He was just a friend who popped into and sped out of our lives in a matter of months. But in that time, something rattled loose inside of me. It simultaneously caused a breaking free and a structural collapse. A breaking free because the part of me that was passionate and full of dreams awakened after several years of forced slumber. And she needed to be roused. A structural collapse because I suddenly realized that my fortitude was nothing more than a house of cards, ready to be blown over by the passing breeze of a cute guy.

I was not who I thought I was.

My infatuation was wrong, so wrong, even if it was all in my head, but it revealed an emptiness in my heart that was much greater than loneliness over fleeting human relationships. I was starving for a real taste of God. Something that would satisfy me. Something that would arrest my heart in pure wonder and joy. I didn't need a new devotional or Bible reading plan. I didn't need another way to reach out to those around me. I didn't need a conference or a book or a friend.

I needed Jesus.

And I needed to know if He really was enough. I'd sung it. I'd shared it. I knew it. But I hadn't tasted and seen and breathed and been wrapped up in it—in His more-than-enoughness.

My wall had finally been breached. This temptation and my own depravity had battered it right to the ground. I had nothing left to hide behind and nothing left to prove.

I was exactly where God wanted me.

In that place of brokenness, God breathed a prayer into my heart. I truly don't think I made it up. He gave it to me. "Jesus," I cried, "I want an undivided heart that is fully satisfied in You!" It became my mantra. I couldn't gather myself enough to even pray for anyone else at that time. I could only plead for an undivided, fully satisfied heart. If God could give that to me, then I could keep going. I could keep believing, keep loving, keep serving. But what I couldn't do was keep striving. I knew that none of my own effort was going to get me that undivided heart. And I knew that until I experienced being truly satisfied in Christ, I would always be trying to fill my gaps with something ultimately worthless.

For perhaps the first time in my life, I was truly desperate for Jesus.

From age eleven, when I was baptized in a frigid Montana lake, I have followed Jesus. I stepped into that water, the pebbles slipping beneath my feet, and said, "Yes, Lord. I'm Yours." That was the moment of decision. I followed Him halfway across the country to go to a liberal arts and Bible college, again saying, "Yes, Lord. I'm Yours." That was the path of learning and being discipled. Then I followed Him into using teaching as missions, starting in bush Alaska and landing on the other side of the planet in Thailand. "Yes, Lord. I'm still Yours!" The choice to follow His calling and serve. Typical stages of the spiritual journey. Predictable and preached about. I had followed Him as far as my faith map would take me.

Now here I stood on the precipice of something unfamiliar and unfathomable. I had missed it in the lecture halls. Skimmed over it in my Bible reading. Neglected it in my book choices. Or maybe I'd simply forgotten it.

I was invited to know and be known by God Almighty, Jesus the Savior, and the Spirit of Comfort. And I mean know as in that awkward know that the Bible uses when a man and a woman get married. It's intimacy at the deepest, purest level. Not head knowledge. It reaches beyond words and catapults us right into the embrace.

I have to say it again: the great I AM was inviting me to know Him and be known by Him. Naked and unashamed. Adam and Eve knew God in the garden. They talked with Him as a friend. Moses knew God—conversed with Him regularly. Elijah knew God, and not merely for all the miracles he did by the Lord's power, but by the Voice that whispered to him on the mountain... more on that in a moment. Jesus, of course, knew God. He was one with the Father, and He invites us into their oneness (remember John 17?), pays the ultimate price for it, in fact.

This invitation to knowing started with my cry for an undivided heart. And it turns out that an undivided heart is God's cry for all His people, too. In Ezekiel 11:19 God declares, "I will give them an undivided heart and put a new spirit in them; I will remove from them their heart of stone and give them a heart of flesh." The Psalmist of 86:11 had this yearning too, calling out, "Teach me your way, O Lord, and I will walk in your truth; give me an undivided heart, that I may fear your name."

It is not just what we believe or our acts of obedience that please the Lord. It is an undivided heart. And He *wants* to give it to us. He wants us to let go of our scrambling after other lovers that cannot satisfy, and He yearns for our full-hearted attention. He desires this for our own good. Outside of Him, there is no peace, no forgiveness, no joy, and no love. He is the source of it all, and by calling us into a deeper relationship with Himself, He is connecting us to His supply.

We cannot find our purpose in serving.

We cannot find our wholeness in human relationships.

We cannot find real rest in media indulgence.

We cannot find lasting joy in numbers of converts.

We cannot find security through a fat bank account.

We cannot find success in whether our children follow the Lord.

We cannot ease our longings with momentary sexual gratification.

We cannot find comfort in a perfect suburban life.

We cannot find the true expression of ourselves in art.

We cannot find satisfaction in food.

Hang on, people. I know I'm getting personal here, but when you've really tasted of the goodness of the Lord, you know that there is nothing worthwhile outside of Him. Your shouts will drown out Peter as you declare, "Lord, where else would we go? You alone have the words of eternal life!"

We cannot find life apart from the One who first breathed life into our nostrils and later bought our soul-life with His blood. It's all in Him. Everything you've ever desired. And more.

But as it was for me, and perhaps is for you, this kind of all-consuming hunger for the Lord was only a nice concept, a stirring worship chorus, until I realized—really, frightfully realized—how useless all of my right things were.

You know those right things. The things we're supposed to do if we're a good Christian. The read, pray, obey things. They're a good foundation, but they're not the source of life. They will not get you over your wall of weariness and disappointment, because they can too easily become religious duties lacking relationship. But all that can change with one whisper.

The story of Elijah told in 2 Kings 18 and 19 floors me every time. In chapter 18 he is challenging all 450 prophets of Baal and all 400 prophets of Asherah to a showdown of the gods. They trek up Mount Carmel and set up their altars. Whichever god sends down fire to consume the sacrifice will be declared the real one. So, the prophets of Baal do their best, chanting, dancing, even slashing themselves to draw Baal's attention. But the skies are silent. Then Elijah, all alone, prepares a bull and lays it upon his altar. But just to really upstage these false prophets, he calls for four jars of water to be poured over the sacrifice. Four jars are emptied three times, until even the trench around the altar is filled with water. And this, no less, at the end of a three-year drought. His actions must have really ruffled some feathers. Then, with a simple enough prayer, he asks God to hear him and to prove that He is Israel's true God. Well, you know what happens next. Fire from heaven. Fire that incinerates every bit of bull, stone altar, and water. This is no lightning strike. This is the all-consuming fire of God. Elijah then slays all the false prophets, predicts the return of the rain, and outruns a chariot.

That's Elijah—big time, miracle-working prophet of God.

Then comes chapter 19. Queen Jezebel doesn't care about the fire from heaven; she's just ticked that her prophets are dead, and she swears to do the same to Elijah. We know from the text that he is afraid, and I'd also dare to conjecture that he was feeling pretty crushed too. He just proved Yahweh's existence with the explicit hope that God would turn His people's hearts back to Him (18:37). Elijah is expecting a change. But none comes. He's still an outlaw. So, he runs. He goes eighty miles away, leaves his servant in Beersheba, and walks another day into the wilderness where he sits down and wants to die. He literally asks the Lord to just take his life. For all of Elijah's miracles, for all of the ways God had used him, he is still human. And like the rest of us, he faced disappointment and frustration in the wilderness. He was bone-tired, and he wanted God to release him from his calling.

But God meets him in this wilderness setting and invites him on a journey. He sends an angel to feed Elijah. Twice. Then Elijah arises, and travels for forty days until he arrives at Horeb, "the mount of God" (19:8). This Horeb is actually the same mountain that is called Sinai elsewhere (see Exodus 33). And Sinai, as you likely know, was where the Lord manifested His presence in a terrifying storm atop the mountain and called Moses up into it to give him the ten commandments. Sinai was where Moses hid in the cleft of the rock as the Lord made all His goodness and righteousness pass by before him in response to his request to see God's glory. Sinai was the place of legends. And as Elijah camps on Sinai in a cave, the Lord reveals Himself in a way that I presume Elijah had never experienced before. First, He sends a rock-shattering wind, then an earthquake, and then a fire. But the Lord's presence isn't in any of these fearsome acts of nature. Elijah has already experienced God in those ways—summoning a drought, calling down heavenly fire.

No, Elijah doesn't need to know more of God's might. So, God reveals Himself in the soul-satisfying way that Elijah does need: a still, small voice. It's practically the sound of silence, but so alive it's just crackling with God's presence. God allowed Elijah to know Him, to experience Him, in a deeply intimate way. It's a whisper. You must be extremely close to someone to hear them when they whisper in your ear. God invited Elijah to lean in and just listen.

And that's essentially what this invitation to know and be known by God is: an invitation to listen. And as we sit still and listen, He imparts the words of life. And those words satisfy our souls in the deepest way. And our hearts become fully focused with rapt, undivided attention on our King. Can you hear Him? He's whispering your name.

Reflection Questions

Have you ever felt desperate for an experience with His "more-than-enoughness"?

What things, outside of God, do you reach for to fill your empty places? Ask God what that empty place is that you're not trusting Him with.

Does the prayer, "I want an undivided heart that is fully satisfied in You!" resonate with you? If not, is God giving you a different prayer to cry out until He gives you a greater taste of His fullness?

Part 6

REMADE

In the happy night,
In secret, when none saw me,
Nor I beheld aught,
Without light or guide, save that which burned in my
heart.
This light guided me
More surely than the light of noonday
To the place where he (well I knew who!) was awaiting
me–
A place where none appeared.
Oh, night that guided me,
Oh, night more lovely than the dawn,
Oh, night that joined Beloved with lover,
Lover transformed in the Beloved!

—St John of the Cross, "DARK NIGHT OF THE SOUL"[1]

Letting Go

I STOOD IN THE BACK of the auditorium with three-year old Rinnah on my hip as the students on stage led the school through a worship song. I spotted Troy a couple of rows ahead of me, a peace-keeping presence amid a crowd of distractible middle-schoolers. He'd been putting in crazy hours to get the school year started well. Hadn't slept much at all the night before. Rode his bicycle to school early that morning. And just kept on giving.

My lips sang the words of the chorus, but my mind strayed into those familiar thoughts of disdain. *Why can't he see that if he keeps going like this, he's going to burn out? Or worse, he's probably going to end up dead from the effects of chronic sleep deprivation! There are so many needs here, I wish he'd just accept that he can't meet them all. Why can't I make him see? God, help me make him see.*

But then, amid my clamoring, a voice. Not an audible voice—a barely-whisper voice. A voice I was just learning to recognize. Yet this time it was so distinct from my own whining tone that I knew it didn't originate from me.

"If I want him to pour himself out for Me in this way, what is that to you?"

I was stunned. Then incensed. *Uh, excuse me, God. But, he's my husband. The father of my children. I don't even have any other family nearby in this foreign land that YOU called us to. Of course what he does matters to me. Of course it impacts me. That's just what I've been trying to get him to understand. Doesn't any of that matter to you?*

But the voice merely echoed again in my heart, "If I want him to pour himself out for Me in this way, what is that to you?"

This time I didn't fight back. I stopped singing, looked at the back of my husband's head and all the shorter heads around him, peered out across the rice fields to where the hills brushed the sky, and I knew. I knew I'd heard the Lord. I knew He cared about me. Cared about Troy, too. I knew He was God in heaven, and I was but dust. I knew His ways were higher than my ways, His thoughts higher than my thoughts. And most of all, I knew I had to let go.

I'd been like Saul, kicking against the goads, injuring myself in resisting the change Jesus wanted to make in my own heart. He had a distinct calling and a new name for me, but I was too busy trying to change my husband to hear it. I'd been caught up in trying to conform Troy to my image; all the while God just wanted to conform me to His image.

Troy's life—and the life of every human ever—is in God's hands alone. God alone numbers our days before we are born. God alone transforms us, sanctifies us, by the power of His Spirit. God alone determines the course of human history. And the sooner I get myself back to that place of trust and surrender to His sovereignty, the sooner I can let go of my need to control or change others.

We must let go.

I would venture to say that a pretty good definition of an idol is anything we are clinging to. It's the thing we dig our nails into and hang on to for dear life. An idol can be a whole lot of different things—money, a relationship, a calling, an addiction, theological rightness or a spiritual gift even—but the common denominator is our inability to truly let go of it. We depend on it for a sense of security. We've all got idols, and in our time in the wilderness, they will be exposed. That's one of God's purposes through leading us into the wilderness, I believe. To reveal our idols. Because when we're weary and full of doubt, we turn back to what gives us comfort. We turn to our golden calf.

We need to visit the Israelites together one last time as they journey through the wilderness. This time, they have only been out of Egypt for about three months. They have celebrated God's victory over the Egyptians who were drowned in the sea; they have cried out for water and seen the Lord make bitter water sweet; they have been desperate for food and been miraculously provided with both quail and manna; they have thirsted again and watched as Moses struck a rock, causing water to pour out; and they have come to the foot of Mount Sinai where God's presence manifests on top in a dark cloud, billowing smoke, trembling earth, and blasting horn.

Only Moses is invited into that awesome cloak of God's power. So, from a safe distance, the Israelites watch Moses hike up the mountain and disappear into the "devouring fire" (Exodus 24:17). He's gone for a week. Two weeks. Three weeks. They're pretty sure God ate him alive at this point. A bit after the fourth week they get desperate. Their leader is gone. The mountain is still spewing smoke, and things are getting real uncomfortable. They don't like waiting in this terrifying setting. Can you blame them?

So, they revert to what they know. "Get up, make us gods that will go before us," they demand of Aaron (Exodus 32:1). They want something they can see. Something that feels a bit tamer and more familiar than this Yahweh of plague and power. A golden calf.

After this idol is fashioned, they lose themselves to it. They eat, drink, play, dance, and sing with such raucous abandon that the hullabaloo sounds like war (Exodus 32:17) and they cause derision from their enemies (Exodus 32:25). The old idol of familiarity and self-indulgence arouses their flesh and they cave completely.

If you don't know the rest of the story, go read it. Read the whole book of Exodus, in fact. Then immediately read the book of Revelation. You'll likely find some startling similarities you never noticed before. But for now, we'll leave the Israelites at their calf worship and examine the idols in our own lives.

The thing about idolatry is that it's so easy to justify, especially if it's not such a blatant sin as pornography or theft. When our idols of security are much more subtle, and even good things in themselves, we are very easily blinded to them. It's that old human ability called self-deception that I mentioned earlier. We're horribly good at it, and we need help getting the scales off our eyes.

When the wilderness shakes our foundations and God isn't guiding us like we thought He would; when we've felt thirsty and hungry longer than we care to remember; when someone who used to give us guidance is suddenly taken away, we cling more tightly to our idols.

My idol was my husband. I leaned on him for security, happiness, and comfort. And when he wasn't providing those things the way I thought he should, I sought to change him. Because, after all, I needed him. Needed him to be all that to me and more. But—no surprise here—it didn't work. When God finally opened my eyes to see that my desperate clinging was causing blood under my own fingernails, I realized I needed to let go. And it took years in the wilderness for that awakening to be ripe. Had all been sunshine and roses, I never would have seen my idolatry.

My wilderness was my undoing, my exposing, and my healing.

Reflection Questions

Ask God to fill in the blank: "If I want to _____, what is that to you?

243

Is there somebody or something you are trying to control or change that God is asking you to let go of?

Do you trust God enough to lay down your idols?

This is My Story

WERE WE REALLY BACK? Back in Alaska? We'd been picked up at the airport by friends who nearly popped our heads off with their hugs. Three years was too long. Matthew and Rachel were there too, and our parking lot reunion was quite the spectacle as Troy leaped into Matthew's arms and they laughed like brothers. Rachel and I hugged an awkwardly long time. I told her I'd forgotten how short she was. She punched me in the arm. Yes, this was where we needed to be. Reconnecting with friends and revisiting memories.

We were only in Anchorage, not our old village, but it still smelled, looked, and sounded like Alaska. I was surprised at how comforting that was to me. The fresh air was tinged with sea salt. The breeze carried the cry of gulls. Fireweed lined the roadside in deepest pink. Hours of daylight remained although it was already past dinner. Something began to stir in me. I couldn't quite put my finger on it, but I could sense a reckoning coming in my spirit.

In that short trip, we spent hours on our friends' back deck, catching up on life. Theirs carried on in Alaska with struggles we could relate to all too well. Ours had moved on to Thailand where a whole different framework shaped our lives. Lives they could hardly imagine. But we were all still *us*, with a connection as far-reaching as the Yukon river.

We borrowed a car and meandered through the miles of mountain, glacier, seascape, and moose crossing that took us down to visit more friends on the peninsula. As we drove, the grandeur swept me in, and I felt as if I was a part of the landscape; like the wild, rugged wilderness of Alaska was a part of me. And then I suddenly realized what I couldn't quite articulate earlier: this is *my* story. All of it. From the dozens of plane rides over untouched lakes to the weary days battling the isolation of the bush. From the scowls of unpleasant, hurting parents to the understanding embrace of a true friend. From the long walks dodging jellyfish on a black sand beach to the days of storm and biting wind that drove us from building to building. It was all a part of me.

So, I claimed it. Owned it. I didn't need to run from it, shake it off, or move on from it. I made peace with it—with all of Alaska, I suppose. Yes, it had been my wilderness, both literally and spiritually, but it was beautiful. And it was a piece of me that I didn't want to forget because, just like the turquoise laced glacier out the window, it had God's fingerprints all over it.

I don't know what your story is, but I do know you have one. God is the master author, and I think He loves a good story—instilled that same love in us. Maybe you appreciate a good movie or get lost in fictional books. Maybe you gobble up memoirs and biographies. Maybe you listen to every online testimony you can find. Maybe you just love the biblical narrative or the parables of Jesus.

Stories are everywhere and, in my opinion, the best ones help us to understand ourselves and God better. Think of the story of the good Samaritan from Luke 10:25-37 (Yes, you know it well, but read it again. It'll do your heart good):

"On one occasion, an expert in the law stood up to test Jesus. "Teacher," he asked, "what must I do to inherit eternal life?"

"What is written in the Law?" he replied. "How do you read it?"

He answered, "'Love the Lord your God with all your heart and with all your soul and with all your strength and with all your mind'; and, 'Love your neighbor as yourself.'"

"You have answered correctly," Jesus replied. "Do this and you will live."

But he wanted to justify himself, so he asked Jesus, "And who is my neighbor?"

In reply Jesus said: "A man was going down from Jerusalem to Jericho, when he was attacked by robbers. They stripped him of his clothes, beat him and went away, leaving him half dead. A priest happened to be going down the same road, and when he saw the man, he passed by on the other side. So too, a Levite, when he came to the place and saw him, passed by on the other side. But a Samaritan, as he traveled, came where the man was; and when he saw him, he took pity on him. He went to him and bandaged his wounds, pouring on oil and wine. Then he put the man on his own donkey, brought him to an inn and took care of him. The next day he took out two denarii and gave them to the inn-keeper. 'Look after him,' he said, 'and when I return, I will reimburse you for any extra expense you may have.'

"Which of these three do you think was a neighbor to the man who fell into the hands of robbers?"

The expert in the law replied, "The one who had mercy on him."

Jesus told him, "Go and do likewise."'

In this one simple parable, Jesus gives a concrete answer to the man's question, smashes social stigmas, and uncovers this man's false sense of righteousness. He also leaves us with a tale that inspires compassion and generosity with the compelling command to "Go and do likewise."

Besides Jesus, I've got a few favorite storytellers, some classic and some modern, but I think my mom tops the list. I certainly wouldn't be typing these words if she hadn't read me thousands of books as a child. Dr. Seuss always made a showing. She even read the whole Bible to me over the course of two years when I was just nine years old or so. The unabridged, uncensored Bible will spark some interesting conversations, that's for sure. And she has this problem with packrats. You probably haven't even heard of a packrat, but where she lives in the woods, they're a frequent source of middle of the night mayhem and accidental encounters with their traps. The poor woman is haunted by the cute rascals. But they at least provide a good bit of fodder for her entertaining stories.

I've been around a few folks lately who love stories perhaps a bit *too* much. They engulf a conversation in story after story, apparently enjoying the sound of their own voice because the listener never gets a word in edgewise. Don't be that person. But do be the person who asks good questions and draws a story out of someone else. Do be the person who readily shares your own story of hope and healing when someone asks to hear it.

If you're not sure what your own story is, my prayer is that you'll take a good hard look at your life and ask the Lord to show you where He was at work. Don't discredit the small changes on the outside that were monumental victories on the inside. I promise you that a change of heart is as big of a mountain moved as a miraculous physical healing. Maybe more.

God has never, not even for a moment, left you to scribble out your story alone. He has been writing and dogearing and dripping His blood and tears all over the pages of your life. You are a walking novel full of hurt and healing, war and victory, fear and love. You are an overcomer who has triumphed over the enemy of our souls "by the blood of the Lamb and by the word of [your] testimony" (Revelation 12:11a).

Grab on to your story, claim God's faithfulness in it, and don't let go. You may be struggling in the trenches of a tough battle right now, but know that victory is coming because you have One who fights for you. One who leads you in the wilderness. One who whispers in the dark cave. The Lord God of angel armies is fighting for you; you need only be still. And when He has vanquished the enemy, you will march forth with shouts of His praise on your lips and a new chapter in your life-book.

As the Lord prepared Joshua to lead His special people, the Israelites, out of the wilderness and into the Promised Land, He declared, "Have I not commanded you? Be strong and courageous. Do not be afraid; do not be discouraged, for the Lord your God will be with you wherever you go" (Joshua 1:9). You, like the Israelites, are "a chosen people, a royal priesthood, a holy nation, God's special possession, that you may declare the praises of him who called you out of darkness into his wonderful light" (1 Peter 2:9), so I think that means God's words for Joshua are also for you.

Be strong.

Be courageous.

Do not be afraid.

Do not be discouraged.

The Lord your God will be with you wherever you go.

And He has given you a story that can declare the praises of Him who called you out of darkness into His wonderful light. Step up, look back, then own it. It's a beautiful piece of you.

Reflection Questions

Is there anything in your past that you need to make peace with and claim as part of your story?

How has a good story or an authentic testimony changed your life?

Is God asking you to share your story in some way to overcome the enemy and encourage others?

Fireweed Seasons

- a poem -

Only a few hardened snow berms remain in the shady areas,
Evidence of Winter's icy grip now releasing the land.
The willow bushes wave their verdant leaf buds,
And the tender shoots of grass emerge out of dark earth,
Rich with volcanic residue.

But where rocks overwhelm the soil,
Where the roadside was grated time and again during snow removal,
Where a fire once burned,
Grows an asparagus-like stalk,
Crowned with a tuft of red and green leaves,
Like a paintbrush ready to stroke a new story across a landscape that once told only its scars.

Sun warms the earth,
Spring rains water the land,
And the shoot grows.

Eager to exhibit the color it knows it holds inside,
It stretches taller, higher, bolder in its calling to redecorate the land.

COLLIDING WITH THE CALL

Every paintbrush bristle separates into a maroon bud, a
gangly splay of awakened desire.

At just the height when fingertips of passersby can dance
on its display,
It opens a blushing face of fuchsia to the sky.
Four dainty petals whisper, "The seasons have changed."
And Summer's countdown begins.

At first, fireweed wears a silky skirt of deep pink,
The promise of days of long sun and sunsets for ages.
Then a river of flowers flows up to its neck,
Telling of the season of red-fleshed salmon and bears that
wait in tumultuous waters to snag lunch as it leaps up the
waterfall.
Finally, the blooms adorn only its head,
As it nods toward the tundra where berries hide their plump
sweetness amid the spongy foliage.

As each flower fades in glory to the newest one above,
A pod begins to form.
Each pod is pregnant with thousands of seeds nestled in
downy fluff.
And as the days shorten and the nights chill,
Fireweed blooms its last.
Fall's crispness startles the sleepy seeds awake,
And they burst forth from the pods,
Floating on a mountain's breath

In search of a place to bear their own blooms in season.

These seeds will find the rocky, choppy, burnt landscapes
in need of life—
A palette to paint their story again.
A story of change.
A story of beauty from ashes.
A story of a Creator who never leaves His work unfinished.

Reflection Questions

How can you see yourself as the fireweed?

Resurrection

IN WRITING THESE MEMORIES, I felt like I was digging up a grave. I grabbed my pickaxe and tore away the sacred ground, revealing roots of where my unhealthy habit of emotional shielding began, scraping up rocks of arrogance and cowardice, cracking open the coffin of my fears. I thought those old fears of drowning under the workload, being terribly misunderstood, failing at meeting needs, and wanting to run away might come alive again and pull me into the grave I had buried them in.

But I was wrong.

Once the layers of my memories were scraped back, I found those sins and fears, yes; but I found them dead and decaying, becoming fertilizer in the soil of my heart. The Gardener of my soul had been at work. All along He was there, breath of life bated in His mouth, waiting for me to expose my vulnerable dry bones so He could revive them with a kiss.

"Who is this coming up from the wilderness, leaning on her beloved?" (Song of Songs 8:5)

Why, it's me. I see it now. The wayward one, clutching her idols of service and productivity, beckoned to the wilderness so she would trade them for fistfuls of the hem of His garment. And I'm hanging on. I'm leaning in. I'm finding my way back to the arms of my first love.

The struggles, the tears, the doubt, the wilderness—it was my undoing.

I had believed He let me go through those experiences so that I would be better equipped for the next assignment, still viewing myself as a utilitarian pawn in His kingdom plan. But it was so much more than that. He was laying the foundation for a relationship with Him that was deeper and stronger than I could have dreamed. I was being reborn, resurrected even.

I guess Jesus wasn't speaking only about himself in John 12:24 when he said, "Very truly I tell you, unless a kernel of wheat falls to the ground and dies, it remains only a single seed. But if it dies, it produces many seeds."

I said yes to a life of serving Him because I wanted to be fruitful. I wanted to yield His glory and multiply His fame and increase His worship. I wanted to see the broken made whole and the hopeless filled with joy. And I still want all those things.

What I didn't realize, though, was that the call to serve was also a call to die. Not just to lay down creature comforts and be willing to move anywhere, but also to walk through the fire of death to self and all that I cling to.

But I can still, with utter certainty, tell you that this promise holds true:

"But now, this is what the Lord says—
he who created you, Jacob,
he who formed you, Israel:

"Do not fear, for I have redeemed you; I have summoned you by name; you are mine.

When you pass through the waters,
I will be with you;
and when you pass through the rivers,
they will not sweep over you.
When you walk through the fire,
you will not be burned;
the flames will not set you ablaze."
ISAIAH 43:1-2

No, you won't drown. You won't be burned up. You will not be consumed except by the all-consuming God, Himself. But you will be transformed. And if you keep trusting the one who created you, called you, died for you and intercedes for you still, you will become fruitful.

Of course, the opposite can be true, too. You can let your wilderness push you away from, rather than into, your true love; and you can become a callous shell of who you were meant to be. But that's not you. I know that because you're still reading, still looking for His fingerprints, still listening for His voice.

Mine is a God of new life, of resurrection power, and of redeeming love. Mine is a powerfully sovereign, yet deeply personal King. Mine is a faithful friend, never once letting me go.

What was planted in isolation, is blooming in gratitude.

What was planted in frustration, is blooming in patience.

What was planted in weariness, is blooming in rest.

What was planted in doubt, is blooming in faith.

What was planted in stagnation, is blooming in creativity.

What was planted in sorrow, is blooming in compassion.

And this place? This moment right here, right now; the pain and the wilderness I walked through to get here? It's my calling. It's the voice of the Lord, alluring me to His faithful heart of love. This place is the invitation. I can see that now, because not a millisecond goes by that is not the invitation, the very call of God.

I don't know what place you're in right now, but I do know this: whether it is marked with joy or pain, it is a call to Love. Will you answer?

"Therefore I am now going to allure her; I will lead her into the wilderness and speak tenderly to her.

There I will give her back her vineyards, and will make the Valley of Achor a door of hope.

There she will respond as in the days of her youth, as in the day she came up out of Egypt."

HOSEA 2:14-15

Reflection Questions

If you are in or have been in a difficult wilderness, what do you believe God's purpose in it is? Now ask Him if He sees it the same way.

How does Isaiah 43:1-2 speak to you?

Now, at the end of the book, how would you define the call of God?

For a FREE <u>14-Day Wilderness Excursion</u> Bible study designed to complement this book, or to receive regular encouragement for your spiritual journey through Corella's blog, go to https://corellaroberts.com

To request group discount prices for ordering five or more copies, please contact author@corellaroberts.com

About the Author

Corella Roberts makes her home in Northern Thailand where she and her husband partner with an international school to "Serve the Servants." They have two full-of-life kids and two chubbier-than-most hamsters. From tundra to tropics, her life of following Jesus has been nothing less than story-worthy, and she loves using her experiences to encourage others to connect deeply with God. You can find her on Facebook, Instagram, or meandering their local produce market in search of mangosteen and lychee fruit.

Notes

Part 1: THE CALL
[1] Chambers, O. (2020, January 14). *Called by God.* Retrieved from https://utmost.org/called-by-god/

OPEN EARS
[1] Hosea the prophet was called to marry a prostitute to represent God's faithful love to His unfaithful people.
[2] Courtney Anderson, *To The Golden Shore: The Life of Adoniram Judson* (King of Prussia, PA: Judson Press, 1987), 391.
[3] Charles Spurgeon, *The Metropolitan Tabernacle Pulpit Sermons, Vol. 36* (Edinburgh: Banner of Truth Trust, 1970), 200.
[4] Law, J. (2017, March 19). *Mandisa Returns With 'Out of the Darkness' Album After 3-Year Depression Battle.* Retrieved from https://www.christianpost.com/news/mandisa-returns-with-out-of-the-darkness-album-after-3-year-depression-battle.html

FISH WHEEL
[1] Simmons, B. (2018). *The Passion translation: the New Testament with Psalms, Proverbs, and Song of Songs.* Savage, MN: BroadStreet Publishing Group LLC.

EXTRAVAGANT
[1] Luke 7:36 – 50

Part 2: TOUGH OBEDIENCE
[1] MacDonald, G. (2020, January 30). *Obedience.* Retrieved from https://www.all-creatures.org/poetry/obedience.html

FIRST LANDING
[1] Kukaewkasem, N. (2017, January 22). *Hope.* Chiang Rai Women's Retreat.

I CAN'T TAKE YOUR FISH
[1] Benton, S. A. (2017, February 6). *The Savior Complex.* Retrieved from https://www.psychologytoday.com/intl/blog/the-high-functioning-alcoholic/201702/the-savior-complex

A PIECE OF PIE
[1] H., A., & McPeek, G. (1991). *The Grieving Indian.* Winnipeg, Man.: Intertribal Christian Communications.

Part 3: THE LINGERING NIGHT
[1] Biema, D. V. (2007, August 23). *Mother Teresa's Crisis of Faith.* Retrieved from https://time.com/4126238/mother-teresas-crisis-of-faith/

GOING BACK FOR MORE
[1] Brown, M. (1892). *I'll Go Where You Want Me To Go.*

BEYOND SURVIVAL
[1] Smith, H. W. (2009). *The Christians secret to a happy life.* Blacksburg, VA: Wilder Publications, chapter 2.
[2] Smith, H. W. (2009). *The Christians secret to a happy life.* Blacksburg, VA: Wilder Publications, chapter 8.

GREAT IS THY FAITHFULNESS
[1] Chisholm, T. (1923). *Great is Thy Faithfulness.*

Part 4: STREAMS IN THE WILDERNESS
[1] Frost, R. (2020, January 30). *Stopping by Woods on a Snowy Evening.* Retrieved from https://www.poetryfoundation.org/poems/42891/stopping-by-woods-on-a-snowy-evening
Jesus

THE WOMB
[1] Hebrews 12:1-3

THIS IS MY BODY

[1] Lewis, C. S. (1996). *Mere Christianity*. New York: Simon and Schuster.

A SHOUTING GOD
[1] Lewis, C. S. (2014). *The Problem of Pain*. New York, NY: HarperCollins.

Part 5: COLLISION
[1] Merton, T. (2020, January 30). *Thomas Merton Quotes.* Retrieved from https://www.brainyquote.com/quotes/thomas_merton_402268

COMFORTLESS
[1] Taylor, J. (2010, January 9). *He Was No Fool.* Retrieved from https://www.thegospelcoalition.org/blogs/justin-taylor/he-ws-no-fool/
[2] Revelation 21 and 22

NEVER ENOUGH
[1] Psalm 23

Part 6: REMADE
[1] St. John of the CrossEx. (2020, January 30). *Dark Night of the Soul.* Retrieved from https://www.poetseers.org/spiritual-and-devotional-poets/christian/the-works-of-st-john-of-the-cross/dark-night-of-the-soul/